The Costume Supervisor's Toolkit

The Costume Supervisor's Toolkit explores the responsibilities of a costume supervisor within a theatrical, opera or dance production company. Rebecca Pride provides an insight into all manner of processes, beginning with a definition of the role, and offers explanations of the timeline from the first design meetings, leading all the way up to managing fittings and final rehearsals. This how-to guide outlines best working practices, including building a team and creating a Costume Bible, while also providing helpful resources such as sizing guides, a list of useful addresses, and case studies from renowned theatrical organizations.

Rebecca Pride is Course Leader for the award-winning BA (Hons) Costume and Performance Design course at the Arts University Bournemouth. She spent 15 years prior to her career as an academic working as a costume and set designer in the professional theatre. Her work at the Arts University has included producing numerous costume-led film projects, including *Wimbledon 1936–1937*, *Storytelling from an Original Point of View*, *Glass Slippers*, *La Passarella*, *Reverie*, *Vampyr* and *Moulin Rouge*.

The Costume Supervisor's Toolkit

Supervising Theatre Costume Production from First Meeting to Final Performance

Rebecca Pride

Routledge
Taylor & Francis Group
NEW YORK AND LONDON

First published 2019
by Routledge
711 Third Avenue, New York, NY 10017

and by Routledge
2 Park Square, Milton Park, Abingdon, Oxon, OX14 4RN

Routledge is an imprint of the Taylor & Francis Group, an informa business

Library of Congress Cataloging-in-Publication Data
Names: Pride, Rebecca, author
Title: The costume supervisor's toolkit : supervising theatre costume production from first meeting to final performance / Rebecca Pride.
Description: Abingdon, Oxon ; New York : Routledge, 2018. |
Includes bibliographical references and index.
Identifiers: LCCN 2018004020| ISBN 9781138182608 (hardback) |
ISBN 9781138182585 (pbk.) | ISBN 9781315646343 (ebk.)
Subjects: LCSH: Costume. | Theater—Production and direction.
Classification: LCC PN2067 .P685 2018 | DDC 792.02/6—dc23
LC record available at https://lccn.loc.gov/2018004020

ISBN: 978-1-138-18260-8 (hbk)
ISBN: 978-1-138-18258-5 (pbk)
ISBN: 978-1-315-64634-3 (ebk)

Typeset in Times New Roman and Helvetica
by Keystroke, Neville Lodge, Tettenhall, Wolverhampton

For Linda Janaway, who taught me how to sew . . .

Contents

Illustrations

FIGURES

TABLES

Foreword

Most people, if asked what a costume supervisor does, would say something vague about making costumes or dressing actors. They might even admit, 'I have no idea.' Rebecca hits the nail on the head when she says in Chapter 1 that even within many theatres themselves, the work of costume supervisors and their teams is a bit of a mystery. With this book, I hope Rebecca can enlighten those who don't know and inspire those who want to know.

I would like to think that here at the National Theatre, the provision of costume is known for its high production values, and all the craftspeople involved in delivering it are supported and recognized for creating a centre of excellence and stagecraft. Often, the sheer amount of work and skill which goes into generating the costumes is underestimated, and many times under-resourced; I hope this book will stimulate debate about the amazing work produced by costume teams.

Rebecca uses a rather useful and symbolic acronym– ROCK – to illustrate the key costume supervisor attributes: Resourceful, Organized, Creative and Kind. It's easy to see the work a costume team produces as the 'foundation stone' of an actor's transformation in performance, and costume supervisors play a pivotal 'project manager' role in the creation of the costume elements. Their primary goal is to 'realize the designer's vision' within the familiar constraints of budget and time. This can be a fierce juggling act to achieve without mishap, and is always a learning curve.

As Rebecca explains, costume supervisors co-ordinate everything, including 'design chats' with actors, sampling fabrics (with or without the designer), engaging freelance makers, arranging fittings, shopping and external hire expeditions, all while balancing the budget. Then, as the production enters the 'tech' week, the costume supervisor liaises with the running wardrobe and wig, hair and make-up teams to ensure the actors come to the stage with all the technical and visual requirements of the costume complete. At the National Theatre, we are very fortunate to work with some of the most experienced supervisors, cutters, ladies' makers, tailors, dyers, costume prop-makers, buyers, wardrobe, dressing and wig, hair and make-up teams in the world, all in close collaboration with the most talented designers. This teamwork is at the heart of the creative process, and key to the work we put onstage – work which is at the forefront of world theatre-making.

We all have so much experience and information to share, and it has been fascinating to work with Rebecca and others on this book and to discuss our processes. The inclusion of ready reckoners for workroom hours, suggested fabric quantities for contemporary and period dress, as well as detailed measuring instructions, really drill down into the working processes of costume supervisors and the teams with which they work. I'm not aware that this information is so easily accessible in any other form elsewhere. This book will be an excellent resource for anyone wanting to progress into supervision or just understand more about the importance of the role in creating costumes for theatre.

Carol Lingwood
Head of Costume
National Theatre, London

Acknowledgments

I am very fortunate to work at one of the most inspirational arts universities in the UK: the Arts University Bournemouth (AUB), on the South Coast, about a hundred miles south-west of London. My colleagues within the BA (Hons) Costume and Performance Design course are passionate perfectionists who have what seem like endless skill in scenography, costume design, tailoring, millinery, costume interpretation and supervision. We all delight in teaching our talented students from the UK and around the world about the magic of the theatre and film industries and the almost constant hard work, patience and commitment required to succeed in these highly competitive fields. So thank you, Mandy Barrington, Adele Keeley, Wayne Martin, Katerina Lawton, Alison Hart, Jon Croose, Heidi Dickeson, Sarah Magill, Helen Ford, Will Hargreaves, Milena Nawrocka and Bunny Winter, who make me laugh every day and give me so many ideas about everything 'Costume'. I also owe a great debt of gratitude to my former boss and mentor, Nigel West, who gave me so much confidence about my work and supported my ideas concerning scenography and costume supervision. In 2016, I was also awarded a very generous research fellowship by the Arts University Bournemouth that allowed me to undertake an extensive program of interviews with professionals and academics from the theatre – so thank you, AUB, for your endless practical support.

Thanks must also go to Carol Lingwood, the legendary Head of Costume at the National Theatre on London's South Bank, who was a staunch supporter with a steady stream of thoughts and information during the research stage of the book and then generously acted as a technical advisor for the project. Carol has been more of a co-author than a contributor, if I'm honest! I must also thank the many supervisors and designers who allowed me to interview them. The countless stories, ideas and tips they very graciously shared really did help me gain a deeper understanding of the difficulties, joys and skills required for this ever-demanding role within the theatre industry. So Lucy Martin, Maria Nicholson, Milly Barter, Frances Tempest, Professor Nancy Hills, Professor Pamela Howard OBE, Amanda Hambleton, Michael Roff and Demi Tarrant – thank you all so much.

Special mention must also go to the super-talented Margaret Maguire and Bill Bradshaw for their beautiful photography which, I hope you agree, so vividly captures the intensity of the costume supervisor's world backstage and onstage. Thanks, too, to Sam Edwards and Adele Keeley for their skillful design of some of the diagrams and illustrations, and their unwavering good taste concerning all things related to graphic design.

I would like to thank the endlessly patient Stacey Walker at Focal Press, who waited for several years while I got the manuscript into shape: she believed in my idea that costume supervision needed writing about, and I thank her for that. Last but by no means least, I must also thank my darling family, Simon, Loveday and Henry Pride, who left me to toil away in my study when they would have preferred me to go with them to the beach!

There is a quote taken from an ancient Chinese proverb that I have had painted on the wall of the costume interpretation studio at the Arts University that I hope inspires my talented students as much as it inspires me: 'Patience is power; with time and patience, the mulberry leaf becomes a silk gown.'

This quote accurately communicates a powerful, but simple, visual image of the combination of creativity and determination required by any successful costume professional – particularly that of a costume supervisor.

Contributors

I am indebted to the practitioners listed below, all of whom gave me some of their precious time for an interview. They have taught me so much about costume design and supervision: some things that I thought I understood, but of which, after talking to them, I realized I had previously only a surface understanding. Little did I know how much information there was to learn and then reflect on.

Milly Barter focused on costume supervision throughout her university course, working on Clare Boothe Luce's *The Women*, *Earthquakes in London* and *The Boyfriend*. After university, Milly started her first job as a trainee for the ITV production *Lewis*, gaining a coveted Creative Skillset Traineeship that allowed her to become the trainee on the first series of *Victoria* for ITV. Milly then stepped up for her next job as junior standby on the Sky Atlantic program *Guerilla*. Following this, Milly returned for *Victoria* Series 2 as principal standby: this has been her favorite job so far. Milly is now working on a film entitled *Hurricane* about the Polish RAF 303 Squadron in WWII. Milly has also worked on the TV show *Quacks*, and most recently covered as a principal dresser on the Disney live-action film *Aladdin*.

Amanda Hambleton graduated from a vocational costume-making course at the Bristol Old Vic Theatre School many moons ago, and has been a freelance costumier ever since. Her work includes cutting, making, theatrical tailoring, costume supervision and costume standby work in TV, theatre and film. Her film credits include *Into the Woods* (Disney), *New Worlds* (New World Productions), *Y Syrcas* (Ffatti Films), *The Christmas Candle* (Impact Productions), *Hyde Park on Hudson* (Hyde Park Films) and *Eliminate: Archie Cookson* (Agent Pictures), and her TV credits include *Will* (Ninth Floor Productions), *The White Princess* (TWP), *The Bastard Executioner* (Fox TV), *Fungus the Bogeyman* (Sky), *Endeavour* Series 3 (Mammoth), *Atlantis* Series 1 and 2 (Little Monster Films/BBC), *Sherlock* Series 3 (Hartswood Films), *Downton Abbey* Series 3(Carnival Film), *Merlin* Series 3, 4 and 5 (Shine Ltd), *Doctor Who* Series 6 (BBC) and *Lark Rise to Candleford* Series 2 and 3 (BBC). Her theatre and opera credits include *Aladdin* (Duncan Reeves Productions), *Peter Pan* (Welsh National Opera), *High Society* (national tour), *Radio Times* (national tour), *Great Expectations* (national tour), *Aladdin*, *Sleeping Beauty*, *Jack and the Beanstalk*, *Cinderella*, *The Wright Brothers*, *Mother Goose*, *Dick Whittington*, *Robin Hood*, *Beauty and the Beast* and the 2015 production of *Aladdin* (Oxford Playhouse), *The Nutcracker*, *Around the World in 80 Days*, *Alice through the Looking Glass*, *The French Detective* and *The Blue Dog* (Egg Theatre, Bath), the Cyprus tours of *The Sound of Music*, *Cats*, *Oliver!* and *The Wizard of Oz* (LTW Productions), *War* *and Peace* (Giffords Circus), *The Man on the Moon* (Travelling Light Theatre Company) and *Wicked!* (Germany transfer).

Professor Nancy Hills was born in a Studebaker in San Mateo, California, and is the Head of the Costume Design Program at Utah State University's Caine College of the Arts. In 2013, she received the Janet Arnold Award from the Society of Antiquaries in London and was funded to take patterns from the historic clothing collections at Berrington Hall and the Hereford Museum and Art Gallery, both in Herefordshire. Her favorite plays to design are period pieces, including *Les Liaisons Dangereuses*, *Pride and Prejudice*, *Amadeus*, *A Little Night Music*, *The Miser* and *Enchanted April*. She also enjoys the process of developing the costumes for original new plays. Nancy gave a TEDx Talk on the impact of WWII on clothing, called *Make Do and Mend*. She has twin sons, Douglas and Tristan.

Professor Pamela Howard OBE is a director and scenographer working primarily in opera and contemporary music theatre. Her practice encompasses large- and small-scale productions in major opera houses and unloved and forgotten spaces. Sustainability and imaginative use of space are central to her work, which links to her former training at the Slade School of Art (1958–1959). A full career as a theatre designer, with a love of text and context, has led her since 2000 to develop a scenographic language of beauty and simplicity onstage, where the performer is always 'the carrier of the myth'. As a compulsive observer of human life, she is never without a pencil and a sketch book, notating the everyday, methodically storing her pencil sketches, and reworking them onstage. Pamela is often the initiator and creator of collaborative projects that link artists from many countries united through art and music. She is the author of *What is Scenography?* (1st edition 2002, 2nd edition 2009, with the 3rd edition to be published in 2019), which is now translated into six languages, and a curator of several theatre-related exhibitions. She is regularly invited to educational events all over the world, and takes great joy in meeting and working with young people at the start of this long journey of creation.

Carol Lingwood trained at Mabel Fletcher College in Liverpool, and qualified in 1983 with a Diploma in Theatre Costume and Design. Her career started at the BBC Television Centre doing alterations and small makes for everything from *Doctor Who* to period dramas. She then progressed as a costume maker and cutter and then as a costume supervisor in many regional theatres, including the Theatre Royal in York, Leicester Haymarket, Swan Theatre, Worcester, Theatre Royal Northampton and the Palace Theatre in Watford. In 1989, she returned to London to assume the position of Costume Supervisor and then Deputy Head of Costume at the Royal Opera House, Covent Garden. This large and prestigious organization brought the chance to work on large-scale productions for the Royal Opera, Royal Ballet and Birmingham Royal Ballet, including opening the new Opera House in 1999. Since 1999, Carol has been Head of Costume at the National Theatre, managing a department of 54 staff and taking on a more strategic management role. The department produces costumes and wigs for over 25 new productions per year, with skills including costume-making and tailoring, costume props, buying, dyeing, wigs, hair and make-up, and running wardrobe support. Carol is also Technical

Director for *War Horse* in China, and is Deputy Chair of the board at the Palace Theatre in Watford.

Lucy Martin's credits as costume supervisor for theatre include *Romantics Anonymous*, *Boudica* and *The Little Match Girl* for Shakespeare's Globe Theatre and Sam Wanamaker Playhouse, *Woyzeck* for the Old Vic Theatre, *Cosi Fan Tutti* for Central City Opera (Colorado), *IHO or The Intelligent Homosexual's Guide to Capitalism and Socialism with a Key to the Scriptures* for the Hampstead Theatre, *The Deep Blue Sea* for the National Theatre, *Elegy* and *The Vote* for the Donmar Warehouse, *Red Velvet* for the Garrick Theatre, Kenneth Branagh Theatre Company, *Macbeth*, *La Musica*, *Creditors* and *The Cherry Orchard* for the Young Vic Theatre, *Great North Run Event*, *One Million Ceremony* in Newcastle, *Crouch, Touch, Pause, Engage* for the National Theatre Wales and Out of Joint, *Mametz* for the National Theatre Wales, *IGNIS* for The Print Room, *Dedication* and *The Nutcracker* for the Nuffield Theatre, and *The Master and Margarita* for Complicité, the Barbican and touring venues.

Maria Nicholson, originally from Reading, England, studied for a BA in Costume and Performance Design at the Arts University Bournemouth, graduating in 2016 with a first-class honors in Costume Supervision. Having studied Fine Art, Textiles and Early Modern History at A-level, Maria's passion for the design and history of costume expanded. Along with her love for organization and thirst for knowledge, further education in costume supervision was an obvious choice. Maria supervised a number of theatre productions throughout university, from Karen Wimhurst's *Freedom, Bread and Peace* (Arts by the Sea Festival, Bournemouth, 2015) to Etherege's *The Man of Mode* (directed by Luke Kernaghan, 2016), expanding her knowledge and skills in the field. Maria is currently pursuing a career in film and television. She has recently worked on shows such as *Father Brown*, and is now working with the wardrobe department on a brand-new drama, *Shakespeare and Hathaway*, for BBC Birmingham (2018).

Michael Roff, while at art college (Fine Art BA and the Slade School of Art postgraduate), worked closely with colleagues on art film projects and performance art events, creating both costumes and props. This led him to work on an ad hoc basis with the English National Opera on large-scale productions, primarily as support for chorus and principal artist fittings, alterations and performances. Mike began a full-time contract with the English National Opera in the wardrobe team at the London Coliseum in late 1985. At this time, the organization was moving into a radically creative period known as 'Director's Opera'. Although these productions could often be challenging for audiences, it was a tremendously exciting environment to be part of backstage. In 1990, Mike toured with the English National Opera, taking three productions to the then Soviet Union. While at the Coliseum, he also had the opportunity to work closely with many world-renowned visiting ballet companies. In 1995, Mike moved across the Thames to join the wardrobe team at the National Theatre. The National Theatre has three auditoriums and puts on around 25 productions playing in repertoire, and each year there are up to 1,000 performances. His initial role was to lead the wardrobe team in the Olivier Theatre, working on large-scale and complex plays and musicals both at the National Theatre and on tour, along with additional visiting theatre companies and co-produced plays. In 1998, his role expanded to

Head of Wardrobe, leading a large team of multi-skilled wardrobe staff and dressers. This role encompasses both the upkeep of costumes and actors' dressing needs, alongside financial and organizational planning and the assessment of technical wardrobe needs for future productions joining the repertoire.

Demi Tarrant graduated from the BA Costume and Performance Design course at the Arts University Bournemouth in 2017. During her time at the AUB, she served as costume assistant supervisor on the Oxford Playhouse production of *Cinderella*, working with Amanda Hambleton. She later oversaw the *Wimbledon 1936–1937* collaborative film, which involved working with over 75 first-year students on location. Demi now works as a freelance costumier.

Frances Tempest has enjoyed a long and successful career as a costume designer for film, television and theatre. She won a Bafta for her work on the BBC serial *Respectable Trade*, and was nominated for several other productions as well as having several nominations for an Emmy and winning a USA ACE award. Her films range from *Under the Skin* to *Calendar Girls*, and television series from *Lillie Langtry* to *Robin Hood*. Her theatre productions include the *Barber of Seville* for English National Opera and Strindberg at the Almeida by way of pantomimes at Stratford East.

Introduction

The principal methodology I have used to research and create this book has been to interview many supervisors and designers in order to build a body of verbatim thoughts and reflections that I could then combine and add to my own experience of working in this wonderful but sometimes exasperating world of theatre costume. One of my interviewees, leading costume practitioner and Head of Running Wardrobe at the National Theatre Michael Roff, succinctly and elegantly described the costume supervisor's primary role:

> *The costume supervisor is the facilitator for the designer. They help the designer to realize their vision: to source, find, make and fit their creative ideas and work into a timeline. The costume supervisor juggles all the availabilities of everyone and everything.*[1]

THE COSTUME SUPERVISOR AS FACILITATOR

The costume supervisor is primarily a manager who leads the costume team and works somewhat in the shadows at the theatre. Very little is known about what they actually do, even within their own theatre world. Not many regular 'civilian' people have a clear idea what the designer does either, so the problem is really quite endemic. To describe their work very simply, the costume supervisor is the person who links every aspect of sourcing the 'clothes' for a production and makes sure the actor arrives onstage appropriately dressed (without bankrupting the theatre company!). It sounds relatively easy, but in reality it can be a highly complex and skilled business, with many pitfalls and conundrums along the way. This book is designed to shine a spotlight on the work of the costume supervisor and to provide anyone involved in the costume shop or outside it (in training, education or professional practice) with an insight into how the costume department interact with their fellow theatre-makers and the creative team.

Unfortunately, when I was a young would-be theatre professional, there was no book I had access to that clearly explained what costume supervision involved as a job. I simply learnt through my many mistakes, first as a set and costume designer, and then in parallel as a costume supervisor. I have felt for a long time that it compromises the profession that there are no comprehensive books about the subject available for students to use, and as a student supervisor complained to me recently in an interview:

> *I couldn't find anything to read in the library about Costume Supervision and it was really disappointing. What I found was always about directing and designing or stage management. It is as if no-one has thought about what Costume Supervision is. You end up learning along the way, making a lot of mistakes that can be an unnecessary waste of time.*[2]

Costume supervision as a profession has progressed so much in recent years, with higher and higher production values and ever more complex technological requirements and possibilities: all factors that have placed more and more responsibility on the costumes to be more practically and aesthetically complex. For this reason, the process behind the work of the costume supervisor now deserves more attention. Generally, the primary concern in costume-related literature relates to the subject of costume design or costume cutting and making. Usually undergraduate programs and courses tend to focus their curriculum on either costume design or costume interpretation (making, or 'building', as it is usually referred to in the US). The result, and consequent reality, is that almost all of those who eventually become costume supervisors have had to learn their craft without the benefit of teaching within the comfort and safety of their educational experience. They may graduate as designers or costume interpreters (or in a completely different field altogether), but will discover through a series of fateful, and usually unplanned, career choices that they are best suited to costume supervision. Students of costume may not even be aware that the role of costume supervisor even exists! This haphazard approach does not do justice to the enormous skill required for the job, and in my view, it contributes to the problem of recognition that is sometimes inherent within the wider industry. Costume supervisors are usually naturally modest people who often stoically work in highly organized, but usually cramped, studios or costume shops without drawing too much attention to themselves. In one of my interviews, the distinguished film costume designer Frances Tempest described the problem to me: 'In a way the costume department perpetuate this myth that they magic up costumes.'[3] As I write this, I can hear costume people wincing at my words of gentle complaint, but it has to be said that costume is constrained by a 'conspiracy of silence'.[4] Are we costume supervisors just shy, or simply not demanding enough about gaining the recognition we deserve? The art of the costume supervisor is traditionally seen in technical rather than creative terms, and as the work is so all-encompassing, difficult and often exhausting, it is my belief that many naturally have no time to record and write up their experiences. It will be no surprise that costume departments are generally dominated by women, and it may just be simple time famine that has prevented these women from recording their working methods. This has always been a problem for women in the theatre, and as Claire Brennan noted, quoting the writer Rebecca West (1892–1983) in an interview with the writer Marina Warner: 'I've always found I've had too many family duties to enable me to write enough . . . oh, men, whatever they may say, don't really have any barrier between them and their craft, that I certainly had.'[5]

Having said that, we are in a period of change, and the digital world has helped enormously, with many informative social media sites, such as the Costume Networking Group (originating in the UK) and Costume People (originating in the US) on Facebook, and other blogs and websites that act as useful conduits for debate and industry interaction between costume interpreters, supervisors, stylists, designers and the wider theatre community. Thankfully, costume teams, led by costume supervisors, are finding their voice to openly discuss and work towards a common professional framework, like that of theatre designers, lighting and sound designers and stage management professionals before them.

STRUCTURE OF THE BOOK

This book does not intend to tell you how to design or make a costume. It assumes the reader already has knowledge and some experience of those areas. What it will do is help the student or young early-stage costume professional to look at their work in a more objective light and gain a toolkit of skills in communication, organization and creativity that cannot currently be found on the market. The book is organized in a chronology that mirrors the timeline of a typical theatre production: pre-production preparation, first read-through, rehearsals, fittings and 'tech week', previews and press night, followed by the run and then post-production 'get out'. Information and guidance relating to production meetings with your fellow creative team members, managing your workload, interpreting the designer's concept, styling and sourcing costumes and handling your budget will be covered, with the appropriate paperwork templates provided. Above all, this book will help you to learn how to devise a method for creating your rail of costumes in a way that your director, designer and actors will approve of and be delighted by. My hope is that by the end of the book you will have a strategy that will help you manage any scale of production throughout your career, by arming you with the measuring, fitting and the sourcing skills that you will need, relating to making, hiring and buying costumes. Additionally, I will examine and describe appropriate and effective communication skills to use when working with your creative team, as you progress from first meeting, to final performance.

The most informative books of recent times (well, not that recent) are by the authors Liz Covey and the late Rosemary Ingham (1936–2008,). These detailed books, *The Costume Designer's Handbook* (1992, Heinemann), *The Costume Technician's Handbook* (1992, Heinemann) and *The Costumer's Handbook* (1980, Prentice Hall), have been a source of inspiration in my quest to discover what makes the costume supervisor and team tick. Another inspiration is British scenographer and director Professor Pamela Howard OBE, author of *What is Scenography?* (Routledge, 2nd edn, 2009), whose iconic monograph seeks to explore the power of drawing and textual research to create a visual and synthesized creative vision for the theatre. Pamela understands the vital importance of costume to communicate ideas, and the centrality of the expert costume supervisor to assist the scenographer or costume designer in realizing their vision. I am very fortunate to know Pamela personally and to have worked with her on several projects. She is a great visual artist and teacher, and I shall be referring to her ideas and creative process throughout.

As I mentioned at the beginning of this introduction, there is so much alchemy that happens in the costume workroom – or 'costume shop' – that no one knows anything about except those who work there. I will attempt to unveil this mystique and communicate to students and those who are currently practicing costume and wanting to learn more the feeling and joy that creating a beautiful, organized and accurately budgeted rail of costumes gives the costume supervisor. Pamela Howard finds words that simply sum up the theatrical potential and energy of sourcing and organizing the 'right' costumes:

> *A set of costumes on a rail ready to be delivered is as exciting as a new collection of fashion clothes, for they are just waiting to be worn. The actor's imprint is already built into the seams, decoration and fabric.*[6]

Throughout the book, I will be referring to a series of carefully chosen case studies of productions I have either worked on myself or followed closely as part of my research. Images of productions and costume supervisors and technicians at work will illuminate the way and contribute to communicating the dynamic and focused creative harmony that exists when the designer, actor and costume supervisor are really doing their jobs to the optimum.

This book will favor American spellings and terminology, although my perspective is primarily focused on British theatre. Table 0.1 provides a brief glossary of terminology (see also Appendix 1 and the glossary towards the end of the book). Templates for documentation can be found on the Focal Press website (www.focalpress.com), and these can be adapted to suit the style and needs of any production, allowing professional costume supervisors the time and resources to create their own way forward with the minimum of fuss.

Table 0.1 Common costume terminology

Please note that most terms are the same in both UK and US contexts, but there are some small differences and nuances that should be defined before reading the book, and these are detailed below:

- Costumes are usually 'built' in the US and 'constructed' or 'interpreted' in the UK.
- It is also important to remember that in the UK, the designer usually works on both the set and costume, unlike in the US, where the two roles are usually separate.

United States	United Kingdom	Definition
Costume Bible	Costume Bible	The file the costume supervisor creates as a comprehensive archive of the production
Costume fitting	Costume fitting	The time when the costumes are fitted (tried on) to the actors during the manufacture stage
Costume sketch/plate/design/rendering	Costume design	The art work the designer produces for the creative team to work from in the rehearsal process
Costume shop	Costume workroom/studio/department	The space for sourcing/making the costumes. In the UK, the term 'wardrobe' is also used, but this is becoming increasingly archaic

Draper	Costume cutter	The costume staff member who makes up the patterns and cuts the fabric before handing it over to the stitchers/ interpreters. The draper will also oversee the construction of the pattern pieces
Dress form	Mannequin	A rigid canvas model in different sizes used to serve as a 'body' when the actor is absent
Dresser	Dresser	Staff who look after the costumes and assist actors backstage with getting dressed and during all quick changes during live performance
Outworker	Outworker/ freelancer	A self-employed costume maker based in their own studio
Rented costumes	Hired costumes	Those costumes that are borrowed for a fee from a commercial company, often referred to as 'costume rental firms' (US) or a 'costume hire company' (UK)
Shopped costumes/items	Sourced/bought costume	Costumes sourced from the costume stock (US) or the costume store (UK), or bought from stores or online
Stitcher/costumer/ costume hand	Costume interpreter/costume maker	The costume staff member who sews the pattern pieces together and constructs the costume itself
Tech rehearsal	Tech	The rehearsals prior to performance in front of an audience – an abbreviation of 'technical rehearsal'
Wardrobe maintenance supervisor	Running wardrobe manager (an older term that is also used in some UK theatres is 'wardrobe mistress' or 'wardrobe master')	The costume staff member to whom the costumes are handed by the costume supervisor once the costume goes onstage. They manage the dressing team and maintenance of the costumes for the run of the show

NOTES

1 Michael Roff, interview and email correspondence with the author, 19 July 2016.
2 Maria Nicholson, interview and email correspondence with the author, 15 July 2016.
3 Frances Tempest, interview and email correspondence with the author, 15 October 2015.
4 Ibid.
5 Claire Brennan,, 'Are women getting any closer to equality in theatre?', *The Guardian*, 6 March 2012, available at: https://www.theguardian.com/stage/theatreblog/2012/mar/06/women-equality-theatre (accessed 16 March 2018).
6 Pamela Howard, *What is Scenography?* (2nd ed., New York: Routledge, 2009), 166.

CHAPTER 1

What Does a Costume Supervisor Do?

Costume has always been an intrinsic component of the live theatre spectacle, because people are always at the center of it, and people generally have to be dressed. As Pamela Howard confirms: 'The human being is at the center of live theatre, and both the director and the scenographer start working from the actor – the most powerful living element in the space.'[1] Even if the actors are naked, or virtually naked, in a production, there will always have to be consideration of how that staging requirement will be managed from a practical point of view, and that responsibility will rest with the costume department, and ultimately the costume supervisor. If the actors involved in a production did not have costumes to wear, they would be without a significant part of their actors' toolkit, and one might conclude that they would not be going onstage as their character, but largely as themselves. Essentially, the designer has the responsibility to create a feasible 'back-story' for each character in the script they are working on, and each decision about each element has to be thought about, found or made and then fitted to the actor. Without costume, the audience might not be able to see each nuance of the actor's performance so clearly and a major element of the story-telling process would be missing or lost. Actors know this instinctively, and the sensitive and wise nurture the working relationship with their designer, costume supervisor and wider costume team.

It is the *live* nature of theatre that makes the work of all the people involved so exacting and complex. Unlike the film industry, where a scene can usually (if not at a financial premium) be re-shot if something goes wrong or is overlooked, theatre has only one chance per performance for success, when all the components will work together in the correct order and at the right time. This harsh reality necessitates a high level of teamwork and rehearsal, and the precise organization of a group of performers by the director, designer, lighting and sound designers, stage management, costume dressers, wig team and backstage crew.

The success of a production also depends on all the theatre practitioners working together for a common *creative* goal for many months and weeks *before* the show opens, with a focused and coherent collective vision for the play or ballet or opera they are working on. Theatre is an artform that is completely *collaborative*, and the work has the best outcome when all the skills of the team are combined to create what appears to the audience a seamless whole. It is only when every member of the creative team learns how to communicate effectively that the performance can have the best possible chance of success. The collaboration should not be seen as completely top-down, with the director or designer wielding their authority. It is far better if the lines of communication flow in all directions, up and down between the team. As Anne Bogart states in Rosemary Ingham's excellent book *From Page to Stage* (1998):

> *In the theatre, we often presume that collaboration means agreement. I believe that too much agreement creates productions with no vitality, no dialectic, no truth. . . . I do not believe that collaboration means mechanically doing what the director dictates. Without resistance, there is no fire.*[2]

That said, it is a universal truth that the buck stops with the director, and as one of the practitioners I interviewed for this book explained: 'It is vital to remember that the director outranks pretty much everybody!'[3] Making sure there is little or no conflict within the creative team requires great skills of diplomacy from all the heads of department, production management, stage management, lighting, sound, scenic and costume, so that the 'fire' Anne Bogart describes can be preserved. Everyone I spoke to in my research interviews reiterated this point: that exceptional levels of emotional intelligence are required by the costume supervisor in order to get the best of out the workroom team and in their interactions with the costume designer and the actors. This book will attempt to examine and highlight exactly what the skills required are, so that any costume supervisor will have the toolkit of these skills at their fingertips for any kind of production.

THE THEATRE TEAM STRUCTURE

There is a very precise hierarchy within the costume shop and the wider theatre workplace, and the lines of working communication are detailed in Figure 1.1. For larger theatres and university costume shops, there will be many staff members, all with specific and defined roles. In smaller theatre departments, there may be many less, with temporary and freelance staff employed when the need and budget allows. It is usually the costume supervisor's role (in association with the production or technical manager) to employ and decide on the team required and then hire them for each production. There may be occasions when you are

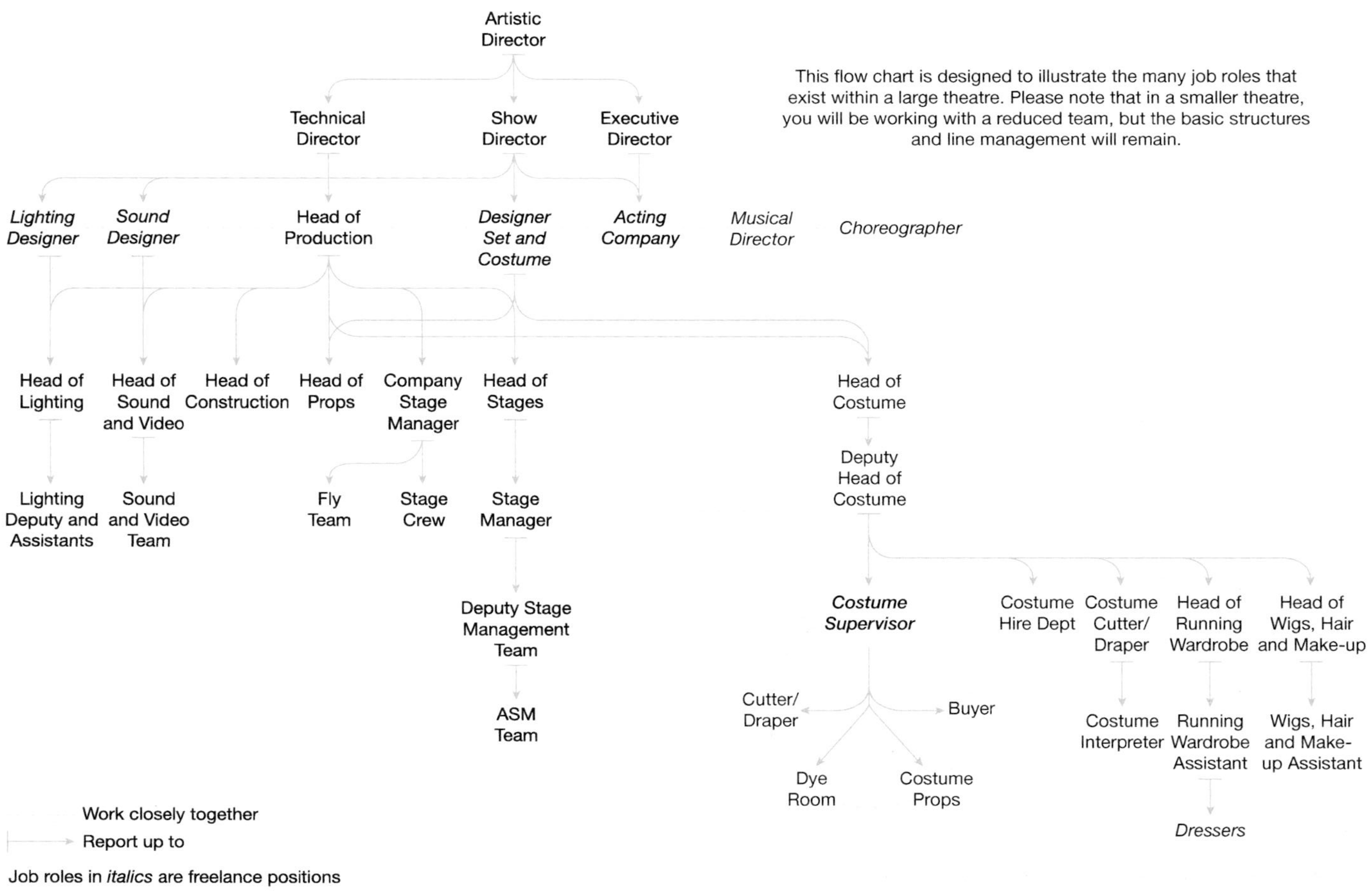

Figure 1.1 The theatre team diagram

Creative Team (Freelance)	Facilitators	Executive Team (Permanent Staff)
Director	Production Manager	Artistic Director
Musical Director	Stage Manager	Executive Director
Designer	Deputy Stage Manager	Technical Director
Lighting Designer	Assistant Stage Manager	Production Heads
Sound designer	Lighting Supervisor + Team	*Costume*
Projection Designer	Sound Supervisor + Team	*Props*
Choreographer	Costume Supervisor + Team	*Lighting*
	Costume Prop Supervisor + Team	*Sound*
	Wig Supervisor + Team	*Stage Management*
	Prop Supervisor + Team	*Wigs*
		Stages

Figure 1.2 Freelance and permanent staff: creative, facilitators and the executive

employed as a freelance supervisor. Indeed, this is the most prevalent employment status. Figure 1.2 indicates the overlap between the permanent staff at a theatre (the executive) and the creative team (who are usually freelance too). The supervisor is placed in the central section as a facilitator. It might be useful to consider Figures 1.1 and 1.2 together to fully understand the lines of communication within the theatre and costume shop.

DEFINING THE ROLE

The costume supervisor's role is to work with the costume designer and the costume shop team in the organization of the building or construction, buying or renting of all the costumes for a production. The costume supervisor is the manager of both human and physical resources. Together, the costume designer and supervisor are essentially responsible for transferring the costumes from drawings in a sketchbook, on a page or in a photograph to actual realized costumes on the stage. This will usually require sourcing fabrics and accessories for costume drapers and stitchers to then make into new original costumes. It may also require hiring, adapting or buying items to combine with existing costume stock held at the theatre. It's a very difficult balancing act for all parties, with the costume supervisor producing and delivering finished costumes that are as close as possible to those imagined by the designer, as well as the director and actors. These costumes also, needless to say, have to fit perfectly. Even if the play or design indicates that they are meant to be ill-fitting, this effect will not have been created by accident. Working effectively with the designer and learning how to interpret their ideas and emotional and creative connection with the production in question requires that the supervisor be a 'consummate tactician; bridging the gaps between the designer's imagination and the costume makers, and between the designer and the actors'.[4] It is no surprise then that the great film costume designer Deborah Nandoolman Landis describes the role in a very useful way, albeit in the context of the film industry, as: 'The managing director of the costume department and the close partner of the designer'.[5]

Costume designers are very busy people, and their workload on even a quite small-scale production can be enormous. If they are responsible for all the major scenographic elements, including the set, props and costumes (as is usually the case in the UK), then they are expected to be a highly skilled architect, historian, draftsperson, engineer, fashion and fabric expert – as well as a great communicator. They are usually too pressed for time to spend days and days drafting fully realized costume drawings, and may well prefer using photocopies from their research material, with lines overlaid to indicate the specifics of their particular vision for the character. Often, a costume designer will only have time to produce an outline of a sketch (see Figure 1.3). When I designed a production of the classic American text *The Women* (1936)

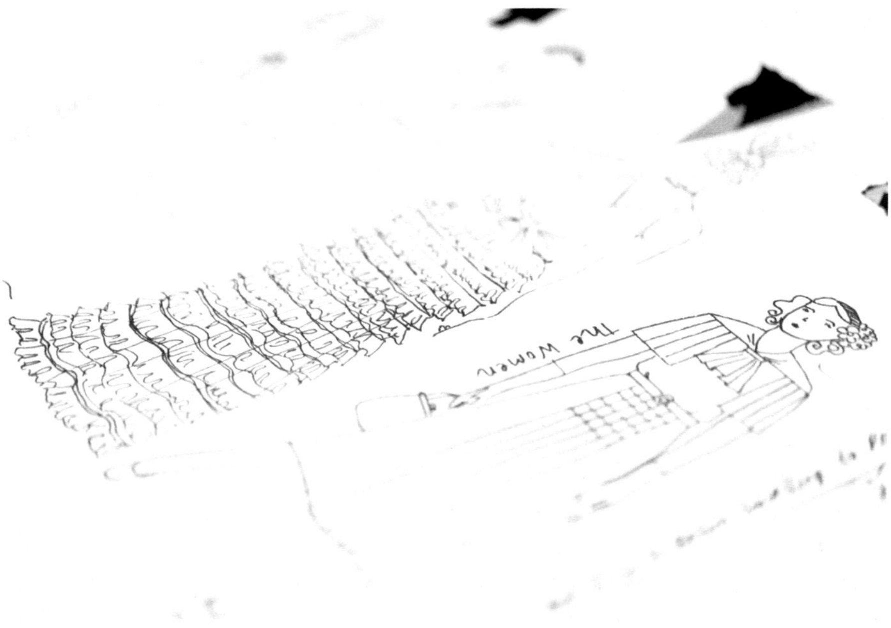

Figure 1.3 Outline costume designs for *The Women*, designed by Rebecca Pride for the Arts University Bournemouth (2014)

Photograph: Margaret Maguire.

by playwright Clare Boothe Luce at the Arts University Bournemouth in 2014, I felt that I needed free rein to decide colors and fabrics on my busy sourcing expeditions, so I simply drew quick outlines, with added photocopies of reference images, for my costume supervisor, Milly Barter, to start to work from. This process was very liberating for both myself and Milly, as we could be more responsive to any fabrics or hired costumes available without the constraint of too many specifics. The play (directed by Gareth Corke, with the set designed by Sam Edwards), is located in New York in the late 1930's, and the all-female cast represent a snapshot of life for women from the very richest to those who look after them as beauticians and household staff. Clothing is key to the narrative, and as the set was designed with a tight color palette, I wanted to respond to the fabrics available when I was on my sourcing expeditions, not design beforehand with strong preconceived ideas.

The designer might occasionally present their supervisor with fully rendered, colorful and precise costume designs that are full of detail, with seam lines and surface decoration fully drawn and considered (see Figure 1.4). However, sometimes the designer will just have the time to scribble on a sheet of lined paper while in a taxi on a shopping expedition: the age-old apocryphal analogy of the design drawn on the back of an envelope is often not that far from reality!

Figure 1.4 Fully rendered costume designs for the ugly sisters in *Cinderella*, designed by Wayne Martin and Amanda Hambleton for Oxford Playhouse (2016)

Photograph: Margaret Maguire.

Some designers may prefer to create a collection of digitally sourced images in the form of a considered mood board for the costume supervisor to work with (see Figure 2.2), choosing very effective ways to co-ordinate all the digital technologies at their fingertips, such as Pinterest and Photoshop. By creating a complex individual style of mood board, rather than the traditional analogue method of drawing every detail by hand, they naturally need to rely on the support of the costume supervisor to help them achieve the translation of their vision from reference sources or minimal sketches through to stage costumes. This often – and indeed should – results in close collaboration, as Carol Lingwood, Head of Costume at the National Theatre in the UK, explained to me:

> *I think a lot of designers see their costume supervisor almost as an associate designer; their right-hand person and trusted sounding board – someone to throw ideas around with. A lot of designers like to work with the same supervisor again and again because of they have this pre-existing collaborative visual and creative shorthand. This can also save a lot of time and money.*[6]

Even if there are no costume sketches available, only minimal or very elaborately presented costume designs, the supervisor must work closely with the designer to provide ideas and to access the resources within the costume shop, to help them style and source all the costume elements. It is an unwise costume designer who does not recognize the contribution a costume supervisor makes to their production, as the award-winning British costume designer Frances Tempest can attest:

> *If you can get a great working relationship, then you have a kind of shorthand when working. You must never underestimate the artistic control of the costume supervisor! Some designers are very hands-on and want to have their hands plunged into the dye vat (me), and others want to leave all the logistics to their team. . . . No, you must never underestimate the artistic contribution of the supervisor.*[7]

The costume supervisor needs to know the production and the design concept and play text inside out: this will become clear after plenty of research into the play in question. The necessary strong lines of communication with the designer require creative interaction back and forth. On a more practical level, supervisors must be able to organize themselves and their costume teams and to be able to plan their time effectively while working to deadlines usually set by others. This naturally requires the ability to improvise, be resourceful, act quickly, keep calm, be adaptable to change and work under pressure. They must also be patient, keeping their counsel and providing a positive approach and a sympathetic ear when the production gets stressful for the designer (or anyone else on the creative team, for that matter).

It is essential that a supervisor has a good knowledge of costume and fashion history, great computer skills, together with a good eye for detail and an understanding of how to create character within a costume. Quite often, the costume designer is not present on all shopping expeditions for fabrics, haberdashery, sourced costume items and accessories, so costume supervisors must be able to know where to find and how to identify an appropriate and authentic costume within the costume stock rental warehouse, the thrift shop, the fabric store, online and on the high street, and be able to delegate this knowledge for the sourcing of these elements effectively to their teams. Indeed, working out this complex jigsaw – where to go for everything and how to approach each new project – is one of the most interesting and creative elements of the job.

During the rehearsal period, the production is still fluid. The designer, actors and the director will make changes, and costume supervisor must expect and even embrace this. On the other hand, supervisors must have the confidence to know when to state that certain aspects of the costume cannot be changed because of practical factors, including the constraints of the budget or the time available to the costume shop staff. Conversely, they must equally know when to instigate changes themselves, without the input of others, if the production requires it, in order to maintain quality. This might involve intervening if a director has agreed to a costume or accessory provided by the well-meaning stage management team that the designer has not seen and which is in the incorrect historical period. It might be that a costume needs revisions for creative, aesthetic or practical reasons, even when the designer is reluctantly agreeing to its inclusion because of time or budgetary considerations. A good supervisor will know how to balance all the logistical demands made by the creative team, actors and their costume department for the overall benefit of the production.

Supervisor will also have the sewing knowledge to be able to keep the manufacture of the costumes on track. However, they do not usually produce costumes themselves – this is the work of the draper and the stitchers. Working with the costume team is an equally important focus for the costume supervisor. Quite often, supervisors will feel as if they are ‘spinning plates’ in trying to manage the procurement of all the necessary items required by their teams in a timely fashion. They must arrange a timetable of fittings for the actors by liaising with stage management (who arrange the release of the actors from rehearsal), and then ensure the fittings run smoothly and that the director, actors and designer are happy with the choices made. They also have to manage the feelings and expectations of the draper and stitchers if costumes have to be significantly rethought following a fitting. Maintaining high levels of diplomacy with everyone can be a very challenging part of the job.

The costume supervisor is also responsible for the costume budget on a production, calculating how much each costume, or set of costumes, will cost to produce, and allocating the budget and staff manufacture hours accordingly. This includes budgeting for the costumes worn by any understudies. Often, supervisors will also have to budget for costume sundries such as hangers, threads and haberdashery. They are also required to budget for all the costume shop staff time needed for the entire production, right up to the technical rehearsal week, and then reconcile all costs at the end of the rehearsal and preview period.

The show is then effectively handed over to the running wardrobe team of assistants and dressers for the technical rehearsal and eventual ‘run’ of the show. If this transition is to be smooth and organized, the costume supervisor must have created a ‘costume description list’ that details each of the costume elements as they are worn by the actors. This comprehensive list is essential, as it communicates to the dressers the exact sequence and order of each costume, increasing efficiency, promoting calm during quick changes, as well as providing specific information that might affect the costumes during the maintenance process. The supervisor must never *assume* a costume can speak for itself!

Once the previews have been staged, the costume supervisor then hands over a 'Costume Bible' that archives all the costume designs, actor's measurements, where fabrics and costumes have been sourced, the yardage of fabrics used, and photographs of fittings and final costumes. If the supervisor was to leave the theatre or if the show was to be re-staged at a later date, this file would serve as the 'recipe card' for re-creating the production.

Costume supervisors also have to be great communicators and 'people persons' because they are working with the actors' costumes, and consequently in close and intimate proximity with actors' bodies during fittings and rehearsals. This obviously requires great sensitivity. There is a wonderful, if rather salacious, quote from the award-winning costume designer James Acheson which gets to the heart of the matter: 'Along with doctors and hookers, we're that strange breed who says "Hello, take your clothes off" to complete strangers.'[8]

The costume supervisor also has to be aware how potential creative indecision by the designer and/or director might cause unnecessary artistic and creative conflict. This reality is usually seen as a taboo – the director and designer are usually portrayed as invincible and pro-active decision-makers who know their own mind, but occasionally the reverse is true in relation to the costume. Quite often, the supervisor has to act as a calming influence and voice with their fellow creative team members, diplomatically dispensing positive advice, expertise, experience and opinion.

There are four main words that the costume supervisor must consider their key goals in communication – Resourceful, Organized, Creative and Kind – and these can be encapsulated in a fashionable mnemonic acronym, so beloved of business management consultants: ROCK (Figure 1.5).

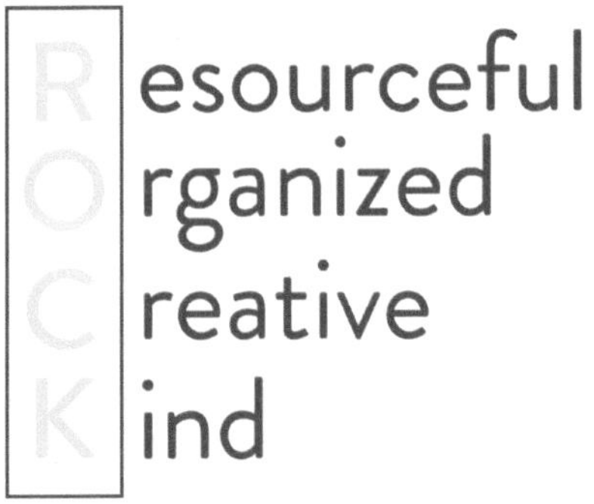

Figure 1.5 The costume supervisor: key elements for effective communication

ROCK also has a rather neat symbolism, as it suggests the literal image of the costume supervisor as the 'rock' within their creative team. Keeping this idea in mind is very useful when facing the inevitable stress that the multitasking nature of the job described in this chapter and the rest of the book involves.

NOTES

1 Pamela Howard, *What is Scenography?* (2nd ed., New York: Routledge, 2009), 156.
2 Rosemary Ingham, *From Page to Stage* (Portsmouth, NH: Heinemann, 1998), 151.
3 Amanda Hambleton, interview and email correspondence with the author, 22 July 2016.
4 Michael Pavelka, *So You Want to Be a Theatre Designer?* (London: Nick Hern Books, 2015), 196.
5 Deborah Nandoolman Landis, *Costume Design* (Waltham, MA: Focal Press, 2012), 188.
6 Carol Lingwood, interview with the author at the National Theatre, 25 September 2015.
7 Frances Tempest, interview with the author at the Arts University Bournemouth, 15 October 2015.
8 James Acheson, cited in J. Kucharski, *Tyranny of Style*, available at: http://tyrannyofstyle.com/about (accessed 16 March 2018).

CHAPTER 2

Different Types and Genres of Production

The work of the costume supervisor may seem relatively straightforward to a costume student or early-stage professional, but the processes and skills are difficult to acquire without experience. There are sadly no shortcuts, and you just have to learn by jumping in! It is important to remember that the basic requirements of the costume supervisor's role are the same for any size or genre of production: 'realizing the designer's creative vision within the constraints of the production budget'.[1] However, the scale of the production can present different problems and issues, so I have interviewed supervisors from each type of show, and will refer to their experience of the challenges and processes they have encountered during the rehearsal, tech and then performance. The three productions will feature as case studies throughout the book, and are indicative of different types and scales of theatre, from the large-scale to a student production. The reader will be able to see how each individual supervisor has handled the sourcing of the costumes in relation to making, hiring and buying for them.

LARGE-SCALE PRODUCTION OF A CLASSIC TWENTIETH-CENTURY PLAY

The Deep Blue Sea by Terence Rattigan, directed by Carrie Cracknell, designed by Tom Scutt, with costume supervision by Lucy Martin, performed in 2016, in the Lyttelton Theatre, National Theatre, London.

The National Theatre is, as the name suggests, the premier theatre complex in the UK, housing three theatres of different specification. The Lyttelton is an 890-seat adjustable proscenium theatre. Directors and designers can opt to make it into an open-end stage, add a forestage or create an orchestra pit for 20 musicians. The production values inherent in the work of the National Theatre are world-class, and the company tours all over the UK and the world with ground-breaking and critically well received productions such as *War Horse* (2007) and *The Curious Incident of the Dog in the Night Time* (2013). The work of this institution might be seen as: 'central to the creative life of the country . . . it presents an eclectic mix of new plays and classics from the world repertoire, with seven or eight productions in repertory at any one time'.[2]

The Deep Blue Sea (Figure 2.1), set in London in 1952, presents the story of Hester Collyer, a woman who has left her wealthy husband Sir William Collyer after falling for a dashing, young WWII pilot, Freddie Page. The pair are living, rather unhappily it transpires, in a lodging house in the then seedy Notting Hill in London. The play and this production beautifully and sensitively present the tragic emotional, social and practical consequences of WWII to a modern audience. The set and costume design served to subtly reflect the intense emotional undercurrents of the story. In a review in the British newspaper, *The Guardian*, Susannah Clapp wrote of the design: 'Lofty, echoing and painted a dull aquamarine, Tom Scutt's design makes the lodging house in (the unfashionable) Ladbroke Grove look as if it has been sunk underwater. In The Deep Blue Sea. Suspended.'[3]

The production could be said to fall into the genre of naturalistic drama with a stylistically abstract staging. For the production, Tom Scutt used an open-end stage configuration. The cast was led by the award-winning British actress Helen McCrory in the title role of Hester. The mood board in Figure 2.2 gives a great insight into the nuanced design development presented by the designer. It is interesting to look at the mood boards and feel the emotional connections the designer makes between color samples and period photographs from the 1950's. It is as if the subtle curation of the images provides more sense of the designer's vision than highly figurative drawn formal 'costume designs' might do. Reading the carefully constructed layers of meaning within the designer's research and presentation of ideas is a key skill for any costume supervisor. Lucy Martin, the supervisor for *The Deep Blue Sea*, describes how she found the inclusion of strong, evocative mood boards in the costume design process very useful

Figure 2.1 *The Deep Blue Sea* production image, directed by Carrie Cracknell, set designed by Tom Scutt for the National Theatre

Photograph: Richard Hubert Smith.

Figure 2.2 Mood board page for Hester Collyer from *The Deep Blue Sea*, designed by Tom Scutt for the National Theatre (2016)

when sourcing for the production: 'I personally find the mood boards used by the designer on *The Deep Blue Sea*, Tom Scutt, are a brilliant way of getting to the heart of the designers' concept for the characters' costumes.'[4]

The majority of the costumes for *The Deep Blue Sea* were made in the National Theatre costume workroom, or were sourced from the extensive costume stock held there. The more than 50 staff and craftsmen and craftswomen who work in the costume department there are all leaders and innovators in their field. There is a team that encompasses women's and menswear, with cutters, costume interpreters, alteration hands, buyers, dye room staff, costume prop and a full wig and make-up department as well as a flourishing hire department housed in Brixton in South London. The costume team also includes the 'running wardrobe', who take over control and maintenance of the costumes once they are onstage in live performance.

CHALLENGES PRESENTED TO THE COSTUME SUPERVISOR

- An historically specific period, which is nuanced with a slight contemporary slant
- A cast of eight principal actors, with an ensemble of six actors who also act as understudies
- A very specific color scheme, which, when combined with the historical period, would naturally require some dye room work and the creation of some bespoke costumes

---

MODERN BRITISH MUSICAL PANTOMIME IN A LARGE PROVINCIAL THEATRE

A modern pantomime of the classic fairytale *Cinderella*, written and directed by Steve Marmion with design inspired by the illustrations of Korky Paul, with costume design and costume supervision by Amanda Hambleton, performed at the Oxford Playhouse Theatre in the UK 2016. The principal 'dame' costumes were designed by Wayne Martin, under the direction of Amanda.

The Oxford Playhouse describes itself as 'A theatre for everyone' on its website, and is a venue for touring theatre from outside Oxford, but this production is one of the few it produced in-house as part of the winter season. Theatres in the UK often develop a specific style and audience for their particular brand of pantomime. To fully contextualize it: British pantomime is a beloved and unique form of musical comedy that presents huge challenges for actors and production creatives every Christmas. This entertainment genre is presented mainly for the delight of children, but also necessarily contains topical humor aimed at all ages. Pantomime is arguably the mainstay of the British theatre tradition, and many theatres and theatre companies rely on its financial success to support other projects throughout the year. Visually, pantomime is almost operatic in its production values, with scenes set in many fantastical, diverse locations, chorus dance numbers, slapstick comedy routines and cross-gendered male and female actors playing the leading 'dame' characters and 'principal boys' respectively.

Numerous costumes are required to be either built, hired or sourced for almost any scale of pantomime. Despite the comedic and 'kitsch' nature of the performance style, the staging and design is taken very, very seriously by all involved. The design of this production of *Cinderella* (Figure 2.3) was inspired and influenced in part by the hugely successful American fantasy drama *Game of Thrones* (based on the book *Song of fire and Ice* by R.R. Martin and adapted for TV by David Benioff and D.B. Weiss), which is, of course, set in a fictional 'medieval'

Figure 2.3 The ugly sister banquet costume from *Cinderella*, directed by Steve Marmion, costumes designed by Amanda Hambleton and Wayne Martin, model Will Hargreaves

Photograph: Margaret Maguire.

world. Most of the costumes were made exclusively for this pantomime, although some were hired or adapted from existing costume stock. Amanda Hambleton, the costume supervisor and designer, described how she began working on *Cinderella* six months before it opened. The workload was sporadic at the beginning, obviously building in the three weeks before opening night. She described the process of procuring the costumes as being epic in scale.

For such a project, the supervisor would necessarily need to be able to juggle several other commissions in tandem, attending production meetings with the director, producer and designer as required. Organizing the making of costumes would follow on from decisions made at these meetings. To do this effectively, it is vital for the supervisor to keep an open mind and present a realistic spreadsheet with costs for each costume element.

For a pantomime like the one at the Oxford Playhouse, the costume procurement process is fluid, and creatively much would not be decided in the first meetings (that took place in April 2016). The content would grow as the script was completed by writer and director Steve Marmion. This would differ significantly from the process on *The Deep Blue Sea*. Lucy Martin would know from quite an early stage the requirements of the classic script and the creative vision of the director and designer. One of the key elements that affects costume procurement for British pantomime is the topicality of the jokes and set comic scenes. These are often written and rewritten right up until the opening night, to coincide with current news, with comedy that relies on props and costume to work effectively. This can necessitate a 'last-minute' and consequently flexible approach to costume that the supervisor must be able to manage in the timeframe and budget available.

CHALLENGES PRESENTED TO THE COSTUME SUPERVISOR

- A short and intense rehearsal period of three weeks
- Late creative decisions concerning costume
- Numerous large-scale cross-gendered 'panto dame' costumes to build within a tight budget
- A large cast of chorus (who are usually children) to dress for the dance numbers (there is usually a 'double cast' for the children, to comply with labor laws for child actors)
- High expectations among the audience of predominantly children for a very visually exciting production with complex comedic scenes and costumes

---

STUDENT FACULTY PRODUCTION OF A RESTORATION COMEDY IN A SITE-RESPONSIVE VENUE

The Man of Mode, written in 1676 by George Etherege, performed as part by the Arts University Bournemouth summer season 2016, directed by professional director Luke Kernaghan, set and costumes designed by students Elle Pollock and Emily Turner respectively, with costume supervision by Maria Nicholson.

The production of *The Man of Mode* (Figure 2.4) was performed at a site-specific, non-traditional space, Meyrick Hall in Bournemouth, in 2016. The play follows the adventures of the libertine Dorimant as he tries to win over the young beautiful heiress Harriet and disengage himself from his former mistress, Mrs Loveit. The majority of characters in the production are wealthy, and their clothes are necessarily lavish. The costumes for this production were made as bespoke items specific to the design, with period-appropriate silks and natural fibers used to enhance and suit the cut of the late seventeenth-century historically inspired designs.

Figure 2.4 *The Man of Mode* production image, directed by Luke Kernaghan, set by Elle Pollock, costumes designed by Emily Turner

Photograph: Bill Bradshaw.

CHALLENGES PRESENTED TO THE COSTUME SUPERVISOR

- The production was designed to fit within the seventeenth-century context, but the director requested that it also had a slight contemporary 'feel'.
- The cut of the costumes necessitated large quantities of fabric, which contributed to relatively high costs for a student/faculty production.
- There were many acting assistant stage managers to dress alongside the cast.
- Finding appropriate historically accurate shoes and accessories within the budget was difficult.
- It was staged in a site-specific venue with natural light, which affected the choice and color of fabrics.

The costume supervisor for *The Man of Mode*, Maria Nicholson, was a graduating student from the course at the Arts University Bournemouth. The supervising task was challenging because virtually all the costumes were made specifically for the production and the director was formally appointed after the costumes had been designed. This is an unusual situation, but one that does occur from time to time, even in professional productions. The student costume designer, Emily Turner, took an historical approach, but with a contemporary influence evident in the form of the fabrics selected. The director, Luke Kernaghan, took this idea even further once the rehearsals began in earnest, by using music, props and movement styles that emphasized the contemporary while respecting and acknowledging the historical context of the play.

All three of these productions are very different, but remarkably similar in their challenges. They all concern classic plays or stories. The costume details for each must be seriously considered by the designer and supervisor.

The Deep Blue Sea costumes are complex because, unlike the other productions, the run is long and the setting would feel more contemporary to the audience, so sourcing exact replicas or vintage items within a tight color and design scheme was a key prerequisite. The supervisor also had to source understudy costumes and manage the complex requirements of the cast, who needed to feel very comfortable with all the elements of the clothing throughout the run of the show. When I observed the technical rehearsals for *The Deep Blue Sea*, I was also aware of the physical movement work the costumes had to be able to withstand. It is not only musical productions that require very durable costumes.

The *Cinderella* pantomime costumes also needed to be built to withstand the rigors of the five-week run, with the demands of dance and slapstick for two or three performances a day. Needless to say, pantomime also has to be a visually spectacular event. To achieve this, the designer and supervisor have to be very creative and work within a tight budget.

In many ways, *The Man of Mode* combines challenges which integrate those common to all three productions. There was the problem of a largely forgotten historical context and costumes that were complicated to make and expensive terms of materials required to build them.

Whether your production is sited in a large-scale national venue, with a cast of leading actors, or a regional theatre, or a relatively small site-specific venue with a cast of young undergraduate actors, the supervisor will face similar challenges. How do you develop good communication skills when setting up your costume team, realize the costume designs as your designer sees them in their head, create a coherent Costume Bible, make sure you source, hire or buy the correct components, manage the costume requirements of the rehearsal process and get through tech week without mishap – and all on a fixed budget?

NOTES

1 Sarah Holmes, *National Theatre Costume* (London: National Theatre Publications, 2014), 6.

2 Ibid., 3.

3 Susannah Clapp, 'The Deep Blue Sea review – an explosive revival', *The Guardian*, 12 June 2016.

4 Lucy Martin, interview and email correspondence with author, 22 April 2016.

CHAPTER 3

Developing Good Communication Skills

The costume supervisor is a multi-skilled individual who, like the production manager, has to be a very astute and quick-thinking member of the creative team. A naturally persuasive person, the supervisor is responsible for so many aspects of the production and with so many different people that he or she has to be a great communicator, 'a people person' and a diplomat, but ideally, also a benevolent leader. Remember the 'K' for 'kind' in ROCK! The legendary costume designer Susan Tsu describes how 'the costume shop can often be the pulse of the theater and . . . actors and techies gather there most often'.[1] It is this easy, calm and comfortable atmosphere that costume supervisors should aim to develop and encourage within the costume shop and in their professional interactions with the creative team, while still commanding a strong sense of leadership and discipline.

GETTING HIRED

When a costume designer is appointed by the director, the designer can usually stipulate which costume supervisor they would rather work with. This is the practice in both the film and theatre industries. For this reason, it goes without saying that smart supervisors work very hard to develop their contacts and professional relationships with designers. To do this well, it is important that the supervisor understands the needs and vulnerabilities of the designer when they are working together. Often during the rehearsal and costume sourcing process, the designer will hear the dreaded words from their costume supervisor: 'It's your decision: you're the designer.' These may seem innocuous, but believe me, they are intensely irritating and passive-aggressive to any costume designer, who, despite months, weeks and days of research, may still be racked with indecision about the minute details of their design. Smart supervisors always put themselves in the designer's shoes and give the designer time to think when they are making decisions, gently guiding rather than cajoling them. To fail in this demonstrates an approach that goes against the grain of the fundamentally collaborative nature of theatre work.

Many costume assistants will naturally progress to costume supervision because a costume designer or senior supervisor has been impressed by their resourcefulness, organization, creativity and kindness, and noticed how they have made themselves indispensable during previous pre-production stages. This is how you get hired: you become indispensable. In the UK, you can also use social media theatre jobsites (like *Stage Jobs Pro* or *The Mandy Network*) as well as all the contacts you can muster to get your foot in the door. Another note to consider: do not rely solely on email, or even letters, to get you work. There is no substitute for perseverance, knocking on doors and making the most of every small contact you may have to help you get to where you want to work. It is essential to become a great networker. However, designers and heads of costume and supervisors can be very busy, so do not under any circumstances pester them unnecessarily. Know where the fine line is between being pro-active and being irritating. That said, costume supervisors are very generous people who remember how they were helped in the early stages of their own careers, and consequently react well to a degree of perseverance, as well as contact that is live rather than digital, so aim to communicate face-to-face when trying to find work if you can.

FIRST DESIGN MEETING WITH DIRECTOR, DESIGNER AND PRODUCTION MANAGER

Once appointed, you will need to prepare for your first meeting with your designer, and then later with the director and production manager for the first formal pre-production meeting. There are several simple steps that you must take prior to these important meetings. It is worth thinking about what your designer's priorities will be. The costume designer will have read the script very carefully to find clues that indicate the hidden, and not so hidden, psychological impulses for each and every actor onstage. Consider, too, the clues laid down by the playwright in each line of text. Try to consider how the playwright wants (or wanted) the designer to bring the story to life on-stage. You can do this best by annotating the script (see Figure 3.1).

It can be great fun and very rewarding to do this part of the job. First, read the script and carefully note down any specific details that relate to:

- any description of character – e.g. age, ethnicity, physicality;
- any description of action in the scene, costume or props that are specified;

Figure 3.1 *The Man of Mode* annotated script and breakdown, created by Maria Nicholson

Photograph: Margaret Maguire.

- the weather and seasons described;
- the time of day and the passage of time (this may not be explicitly described – you may have to work it out);
- any obvious quick changes or any potential special effects – e.g. blood stains, actors who need to be 'flown' by harness, or physical changes, including pregnancy.

It is important to remember that the playwright may omit specific details in the stage directions, only including important information in the narrative spoken by the actors. These slips in stage direction are easily missed, so read slowly and carefully. It is a good idea to create an initial 'preliminary costume plot' after annotating the script, as this will keep all the details clear, which will in turn help you to successfully manage your first meeting with the designer.

Write all over the script as necessary using markers and highlighter pens, and scribble your thoughts in pencil (see Figure 3.2). Use anything that comes to hand. Fold back important pages so that you don't overlook them later on. Think laterally: is the description you are reading indicative of a costume problem? Be aware that your designer and director may well have very different ideas about this production than the author. One thing is for sure, though: you must go to that first meeting fully aware of the basic requirements of the play you are working on. It is important to remember that working through the script will take time – enjoyable time for sure – but it should take you several hours.

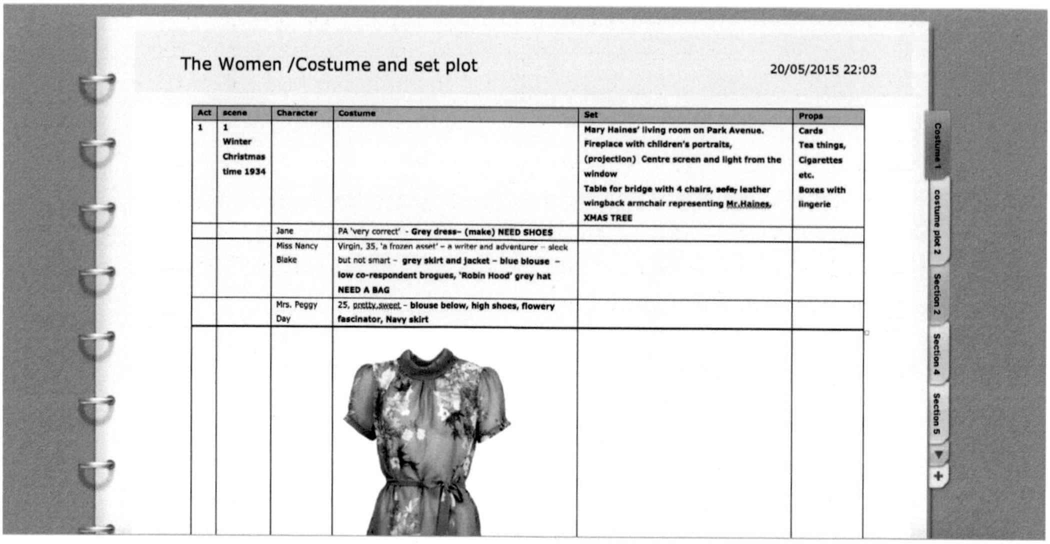

The Women /Costume and set plot 20/05/2015 22:03

Act	scene	Character	Costume	Set	Props
1	1 Winter Christmas time 1934			Mary Haines' living room on Park Avenue. Fireplace with children's portraits, (projection) Centre screen and light from the window Table for bridge with 4 chairs, ~~sofa,~~ leather wingback armchair representing Mr.Haines, XMAS TREE	Cards Tea things, Cigarettes etc. Boxes with lingerie
		Jane	PA 'very correct' - Grey dress– (make) NEED SHOES		
		Miss Nancy Blake	Virgin, 35, 'a frozen asset' – a writer and adventurer – sleek but not smart – grey skirt and jacket – blue blouse – low co-respondent brogues, 'Robin Hood' grey hat NEED A BAG		
		Mrs. Peggy Day	25, pretty.sweet - blouse below, high shoes, flowery fascinator, Navy skirt		

Figure 3.2 Screenshot of the author's preliminary costume and set plot from *The Women*

It is also a good idea to do a basic Google search on the playwright, the script and previous productions of the play. Before the Internet, this was quite an onerous task to undertake, but nowadays there is absolutely no excuse for being underprepared. Again, it is good to remember that all the research you do may conflict with the eventual vision of the director and designer. However, on hearing your ideas and realizing you have a good working understanding of the script, your collaborators will both be pleased and reassured that they have a costume supervisor on board who takes the production as seriously as they do.

POINTS TO CONSIDER WHEN RESEARCHING THE SCRIPT

- What was the date of the original opening production of the play?
- Does the play relate to a specific historical/period context?
- Are there any notable previous productions of your play that you should consider?

If you are working with a designer or director for the first time, it is imperative that you take an hour or two to familiarize yourself with their work and creative style. Have they worked together before, and if so, what was the style of their previous work? Will their working practices influence your approach to the first meeting? Research reviews of their work in journals and newspapers. If they have a production on-stage that you can see before your meeting, then do go and see it. This will help you with small/shop talk when you first meet and give you insight into their creative style and previous successes (and those productions that were less so). This sort of research is so easy to do nowadays with the Internet at your fingertips, and it will pay dividends later on.

If you are working in an undergraduate or graduate setting, effectively as an unpaid amateur costume supervisor, it is unlikely you will have been chosen by your designer. The same principles apply when you prepare for your first production meeting with the creative team. You may even be expected to complete even more detailed research than a seasoned professional (who has to work in a tighter time frame by economic necessity).

LISTENING

At the first creative meeting, it is important to take time to *listen*. You can learn as much from 'active' listening as from speaking. It is also important to remember that the director and designer are very busy people, so contribute to the conversation after thinking about what you are going to say. I often like to remind myself that 'listen' and 'silent' are words that contain the same letters! As Amanda Hambleton explained to me in relation to her meetings for the production of *Cinderella*:

> *Make sure you listen to everybody and remember there is usually a set way to conduct the meeting in an organized way. Each department should have their say. Wait for your moment to add your information. Be respectful of other departments. Everyone is pressed for time, so understand this. Say just what must be said.*[2]

Your first meeting will usually have quite specific agenda. If the production manager attends, they will usually act as the chair of the meeting. The agenda will usually work as shown in Table 3.1.

If you are an experienced costume supervisor, you would ideally have prepared an initial costume budget based on your first reading of the script and perhaps an understanding of the creative style of the director and designer. If you are working for the first time as a student costume supervisor, it is important to take extensive notes and to gain an idea of the overall budget for costumes as outlined by the production manager and director or designer. At this stage, do not be afraid to voice concern if you think that insufficient budget has been allocated to costume. Sometimes, because set is often the largest element in the in the visual picture, it can be seen by the producers and production managers as the most obviously expensive item. There are many reasons for this, and I briefly touched on the problem in the Introduction when discussing how costume is often misunderstood even within the theatre itself. It is the duty of the costume supervisor to fully explain and advocate for their costume budget. You can only do this effectively if you have prepared your script breakdown and initial costing sheet with a tally of the number of costumes that appear to be required. Fortunately, insufficient costume budget is not a situation that occurs at the National Theatre. Indeed, in conversation with Carol

Table 3.1 Pre-production meeting agenda

Pre-production Meeting Agenda	
Date:	
Director:	
Designer:	
Production Manager:	
Item	Notes
1. Overall Concept and Ideas for the Production	
2. Length of Run/Number of Performances	
3. Dates for the Run/Tour (If Relevant)	
4. Rehearsal Venue Location and Dates	
5. Casting Status	
6. Music (If Relevant)	
7. Choreography (If Relevant)	
8. Costume and General Props	
9. Costume	
10. Lighting	
11. Sound	
12. Stage Management	
13. Budget	
14. Future of the Production	

Lingwood, it was very clear that the reverse is sometimes true, with the set, lighting, sound and prop departments often allocated less!

Take time to fully absorb the requirements of the set after the designer presents their initial ideas. What is the style? Is there a specific color scheme that is the focus of the design scheme, as was evident in *The Deep Blue Sea*? Will the color scheme have a bearing on the costume design and associated costs? Think about how the actors will be using the set. In *The Deep Blue Sea*, the designer, Tom Scutt, used multiple levels, effectively bisecting a whole London terraced house laterally through the middle (see Figure 2.1). Ensemble actors could be seen travelling up and down the staircase visible through the transparent walls of the set, to the three levels. Immediately upon seeing the design, supervisor Lucy Martin was alerted to the fact that she had to consider the color and silhouette of the costumes lit through the gauze flattage. She also prepared for the fact that the actors' footwear would need to be durable and non-slippery on the stage steps, or 'treads'. In the initial meetings for *Cinderella*, Amanda Hambleton considered the overall concept for the production and looked for direction about how the pantomime would reflect and be influenced in design terms by the illustration work of Korky Paul and the underlying influence of *Game of Thrones* and medieval fantasy realism. The design for *The Man of Mode* was inevitably modified to accommodate the site-specific space at Meyrick Hall, which has limited theatre lighting and natural daylight. Brighter and more textured fabrics were chosen to make the most of the natural lighting conditions and the close proximity of the audience 'in traverse'.

If you have a knowledge of the costume stock available at the theatre you are working in, then you should offer ideas about how these potential costumes may fit into the scheme presented to you. Your production manager, who has oversight of the production from a logistical and financial point of view, will be very interested to hear how many costumes are required, and which costumes will be the most expensive to produce or have difficult technical requirements that may need to be resolved prior to the beginning of the rehearsal period. If you have done your homework, the production manager is more likely to allocate you a sensible budget for costume because you have made a case for appropriate funds.

After the meeting, take a few minutes to look over your notes. If the designer is available, discuss where and when you will next be meeting and summarize your ideas for your strategy going forward. Your next challenge will be to confirm your own contract, if you are freelance (see Chapter 5), and then meet with the costume shop team. If you are a permanent member of costume staff, then you will now go back to meet with your drapers and stitchers to discuss the new production. Take plenty of time now to make more notes and plan and think things through before you begin the challenge of getting your costumes into the build stage of production, and then on a rail.

NOTES

1 Susan Tsu, 'Foreword', in Rosemary Ingham and Liz Covey, *The Costume Technician's Handbook* (Portsmouth NH: Heinemann, 1992).

2 Amanda Hambleton, interview and email correspondence with the author, 22 July 2016.

CHAPTER 4

Setting up Your Team

As a costume supervisor, you are a manager of people and resources. Theatre is a completely collaborative artform, and as discussed in previous chapters, you cannot do your job properly if you do not reflect on this undeniable truth. You have to work with others to get the best possible outcome: this is part of the joy of theatre and costume, but it requires a high level of management skill. The job role is summarized below, and reads quite simply as a list; however, it is more easily written than enacted:

- collaborating (working with the designer, director, production manager, actors and costume shop);
- listening (to all of the above);
- preparing (for meetings with the director and design and for fittings);
- managing (the procurement and building of the costumes);
- budgeting (for each and every costume element, including the 'consumables' for the run of the show (that's every extra item required to stage the show e.g. tights, extra copies of costumes that may have added wear and tear and then need replacing);
- maintaining a positive and creative environment in the costume shop.

Sometimes the costume supervisor may have a large team, each with clearly designated responsibilities. Or, as is quite common nowadays, the supervisor may be on their own: a costume supervisor who does almost everything, with a few casual or freelance stitchers employed when required, to relieve the strain of reaching deadlines for fittings, the tech and dress rehearsals.

LEADERSHIP

The department might be big or small, but either way, it is always very useful to examine which style of leadership you favor in your work as a costume supervisor. Les McKeown, in his insightful book *Do Lead*, outlines some of the problems faced when considering ideas of leadership: 'we see it as an elite act, set apart from everyday life and undertaken by people who are somehow special. That leadership is something "other", something practiced by people who are not you, not I.'[1]

Quite often in costume, we run at the job quite frantically and barely get the time to think about how we tend to approach our work. However, no matter how busy you are and the deadlines you have to face, try to consider how you prefer to get things done. As we have established already, costume supervisors have to be forensically organized, resourceful and able to work with so many different people with different needs, both practical and creative. Within the same hour, you may be discussing the problems of staging a difficult quick change with an actor, director and stage manager, a complex historical detail with a designer, the problem of finding the right underwear or shoes for an actor, or how to source the correct textile effect on an awkward fabric with your costume dyer. That is quite a feat of logistical and creative gymnastics to perform.

The supervisor will also be juggling staff hours, human resources, health and safety needs and rules, expenses and budgets. The job of managing all this is both creative and mundane at the same time. However, working with so many different people can be challenging, but facing this is, in essence, the key to understanding management. You will need to learn and develop strategies for quickly assessing any situation and be able to size up the individual problems that each new job or production will present you with. You are working in a small world in the theatre, where your approach will be scrutinized and remembered, so you will need to find considered resolutions to any conflicts that arise. Listen to others, and seek advice from your manager or executive team if you need to. Asking for help is never a sign of weakness. You may work as a permanent member of staff or freelance. If you are the former, you will hopefully be working with an established team, and the potential conflicts or challenges may come from the other creatives (director, designer or actors). If you are freelance, then you will need to swing right into action straight away once you begin work, being receptive to your team and judging how best to work with them to produce your new show.

Look at your team of established permanent staff and speak to each member individually to discover their specific strengths. This will give you the opportunity to explain how you like to work and what is important to you in relation to this particular production. It is always a good idea to try to see yourself as others see you, and if you should encounter a resistant team member, then attempt to unravel why they are behaving or reacting in a certain way. Most costume shops are full of people who usually work too hard, or are perfectionists who do almost too much and can be their own harshest critics. This can be stressful and awkward to manage, but by setting clear targets, you will begin to alleviate this. By the same token, a freelance costume supervisor who comes into a costume shop and micro-manages too much can be unwelcome. You must set clear targets in terms of time, output and quality. Do this with the minimum of fuss and with absolute clarity, and you should find your approach to management is appreciated by your team. Nancy Hills, a costume designer from the United States, reiterated during our interview the importance for her of working in a pleasant and democratic environment in the costume shop:

> *Supervisors have so many different techniques and ways of working: there is no complete consensus. I know the environment I want to work in. I want to work in a nurturing situation. . . . It should not be a didactic environment. It is so easy for the costume shop to become a sweat shop and that is really counter-productive, as then you don't all get to fully share in the joy of creating this piece of art . . .*[2]

If you are working at a large theatre, you may need to appoint freelance costume staff to build costumes alongside the existing drapers and stitchers. Your previous pre-production meeting with the designer will have alerted you to the requirements and priorities for the production. Take stock and decide which of your network of freelancers you will approach to make what costume. If you are new to the costume shop as a freelance, then consulting with the draper will provide you precious knowledge about the specific strengths and skills of the costume shop staff. Always match costume 'builds' to staff expertise: don't expect a maker to go against the grain of their particular skillset, unless you want them to be unhappy and miserable!

There is no great mystique to being the leader of a team. Understand and think about what your objectives are, and act on them. Try to minimize conflict or misunderstanding through effective and unambiguous communication with everyone, and believe in yourself and your capacity to lead. Then all should be well.

COSTUME ROLES AND RESPONSIBILITIES

Each role in the shop has its own specific responsibilities, with you, the costume supervisor, at the top of the pyramid. Table 4.1 details the basic job description and duties for each role.

A costume shop is usually a very busy and frenetic place, with highly skilled craftspeople working together, using many different materials, to create what is hopefully an integrated, authentic, exciting and theatrically creative response to a text. The staff within the costume shop often endure long hours and perform work that is very physically and intellectually demanding to support the designer's vision. Naturally, they are very dedicated to their individual job roles. A costume shop should not really be seen as a factory: the work that is being made there is not comparable with the garments made in a fashion house. As the great costume

Table 4.1 Costume shop/workroom job roles

Role	Job description	Duties
Assistant supervisor/ deputy	The assistant supervisor/deputy works closely with the supervisor to collect and source costumes for the production they are assigned to work on. The assistant supervisor may also prepare the 'costume description list' ready for the running wardrobe team and do some of the shopping for the production	They work to support the supervisor and all other members of the costume team during the pre-production period and tech week They will work with the supervisor to make sure fittings with actors are managed successfully and run smoothly
Buyer	The buyer, as the name suggests, is responsible buying for the production, and will be responsible for purchasing materials and goods in respect of costumes, footwear and accessories, using a wide range of sources and suppliers, retail and wholesale, in accordance with the designer's vision and the supervisor's instruction	The buyer takes instruction from the supervisor and makes detailed shopping lists prior to a sourcing trip The shopping excursions can be complex, and the buyer has to be very organized and able to cope with stressful situations, as well as having high levels of physical endurance to cope with the carrying and long days travelling around town Common sense and quick thinking are also important, since the designer and supervisor are often absent from these excursions as they are working back at the theatre with the actors and director
Costume draper/ cutter	The draper/cutter works from the costume designs to create patterns for any costumes that are to be made It goes without saying that the draper/ cutter is a very highly skilled individual who is expected to have a vast knowledge of all historical periods of clothing and the appropriate construction methods	The draper/cutter cuts the fabric supplied by the costume supervisor and hands it to the stitchers/workroom assistants to make up the costumes, including all linings, facings etc They manage the process of manufacture in association with the costume supervisor and designer, giving detailed instruction to the other costume shop staff
Costume prop maker	Costume props are any costumes that require mastery of a wider range of materials and techniques. An example of a costume prop might be a two-man pantomime horse, or a costume for a giant character that requires a complex understructure to add height. The costume prop maker will also create jewelry, hats and accessories	They work with complex materials and specialist tools to create unusual costumes from the designer's brief

Role	Job description	Duties
Dye room staff	The dye room team dye fabric, usually before it is cut, but sometimes after the costume is constructed. They are also responsible for printing fabrics, dyeing shoes and accessories, preparing unusual textiles and creating devoré fabrics	They maintain an organized dye space and plan the dye process for each project safely and on time They may 'finish' the costume by subtly ageing it, known as 'breaking it down'
Stitchers/ workroom staff	The stitcher assembles and manufactures the costumes as instructed by the draper/ cutter	They create the final costume to a high standard They must maintain a tidy and organized workroom

designer, curator and academic Professor Deborah Nandoolman Landis explained when she delivered a highly insightful keynote lecture at the Arts University in 2006:

> *Costumes are defined by what they are not. Costumes are not fashion; they do not exist to serve to promote a designer label or line. Costume design is not an entrepreneurial profession; we do not sell the clothes we design.*[3]

This is an important distinction of costume work.

Entering the 'hot house' that is the costume shop can be a little daunting for the free-lance costume designer. As a supervisor, it is a good idea to be aware of this and develop a quick and warm conviviality, while still demonstrating, with actions rather than words, your own work ethic and professionalism. Introduce your designer to the team one by one. Much misunderstanding can occur if this process is mishandled. Costume drapers, buyers and stitchers are collaborating with the designer, not just 'working for' them. Occasionally, costume makers can feel a certain unspoken powerlessness while waiting for their designs and fabrics to arrive: disperse this feeling by communicating clearly, and everyone will be happy and feel creatively linked to the ultimate endgame of producing beautiful and well-fitted costumes. Lucy Martin, supervisor for *The Deep Blue Sea*, explained succinctly the primary focus of the costume supervisor's work: 'Essentially your job is to make sure the actors have something appropriate to wear onstage . . . and to work collaboratively with the costume makers to ensure that, together, you are using and realizing the same references . . .'[4]

Getting sight of the costume designs for the first time (as on the *Cinderella* pantomime – see Figure 4.1), is an exciting time for the costume team, but also a time when you as the supervisor need to be sensitive and focused. Once the designer delivers their designs, sit down with your assistant or draper to discuss the costumes in detail before they are allocated to your team for fabric sourcing and then making. This could be the moment when the ubiquitous British cup of tea comes in very handy! Always try to maintain the warm, convivial atmosphere mentioned in Chapter 3, with the costume shop as the center of the theatre.

Figure 4.1 Looking at the costume designs for the first time, *Cinderella*, Oxford Playhouse

Photograph: Margaret Maguire.

Once you have taken time to acquaint yourself with how the costume shop operates, the supervisor will begin the process of establishing deadlines for the production period. The supervisor needs to include the costume designer in this process, as the designer may be working on several productions at the same time and have limited availability. Awkward dates for fittings and consequently deadlines may affect budgeting, so setting dates early is essential. Actors cannot usually be available at short notice, so the supervisor should consult with the stage management team for mutually agreed fitting times.

Sometimes directors may be reluctant to designate time for fittings – this can be a point of friction if not managed or planned with sensitivity. The efficient costume supervisor will need great skills in diplomacy to co-ordinate the needs of the actor, director, costume designer and the rehearsal schedules with those of outworkers and the in-house staff. Organizing an achievable timeline for the sourcing and dyeing of fabrics for makers, ordering bespoke items like shoes or millinery is also your main priority at this stage. Planning the sourcing of costume items that are needed in the rehearsal room (in advance of arriving at the theatre) will also need to be considered.

SETTING UP THE FINANCE AND CASH FLOW FOR YOUR PRODUCTION

So far, this chapter has focused on the costume supervisor's role within an established costume department or shop. This may not always be the situation facing the supervisor. For the Oxford Playhouse production of *Cinderella* (2016), freelancer Amanda Hambleton was contracted to provide her own space and to arrange every detail of sourcing the costume herself. In this situation, it is essential to agree the financial parameters for your contract in the initial stages of discussion with the producers. You must deal with the difficult area of money and cash flow before you do anything else. This is very, very important!

Be astute, and consider these basic elements and conditions:

- Define in conversation with your producers exactly what you are responsible for.
- Do you have a space to work in? If not, will the producer be paying upfront for the hire of space and equipment?
- Will you be reimbursed for use of your personal transport, cell phone, home telephone, printing, packing and shipping of the costumes or goods?
- Who will be responsible for the overall delivery of the costumes to the first venue?
- Who will be the person to allocate and handle expenses for the costume team?
- Who will be responsible for public liability insurance for the team and yourself?

Next, as a supervisor, you will need to work out how to physically access the budget. If freelance, it is unadvisable to begin work on anything if these points have not been resolved and detailed within your contract. Carol Lingwood warned: 'Be mindful that you need to work out every aspect of accessing the budget before you begin work.'[5]

If the supervisor is freelance, it is usual to be paid though a system of scheduled payments. There might be two or three stages of payment. You might agree to half the budget upfront as you begin work, with the final payment on completion of the technical week and the handover of the Costume Bible. Alternatively, for a longer project, you might be paid one third upfront on signing your contract, before rehearsals begin, then with staged payments at pre-agreed intervals: first fitting and then reconciliation of the budget after the first night of the production (see the example of a costume supervisor's contract in Appendix 2).

It is a very good idea, whether freelance or a permanent staff member, to set up a bank account and credit card just for your work finances. As Carol Lingwood also recommended: 'A headline message to a freelance supervisor is to keep your work finance and personal finance separate.'[6] Some larger theatres may even issue you with a credit card once you have signed your contract and begun work. This is the ideal situation as your personal finances are then completely separate. Naturally, you will be required by the head of costume or production manager to keep very accurate spreadsheets that include your company credit card spending. It is vital that you never start working on a production until you have settled all the questions listed above and have the finance information and your contract signed and the money in the bank, no matter how soon the deadline is for getting this show onstage . . .

NOTES

1 Les McKeown, *Do Lead – Share Your Vision. Inspire Others. Achieve the Impossible* (London: The Do Book Company, 2014), 9.
2 Nancy Hills, interview with the author at the Arts University Bournemouth, June 2016.
3 N. West, V. McClean and M. Stender (Eds), *Costume Symposium 2006* (Bournemouth: The Arts Institute, 2006), 15.
4 Lucy Martin, interview with the author at the National Theatre, April 2016.
5 Carol Lingwood, interview with the author at the National Theatre, April 2017.
6 Ibid.

C H A P T E R 5

Budgeting

When the contract details are settled and signed, and access to funds has been agreed, then there are several processes that relate to setting up a working budget. Your production manager or head of costume (if you are working in a larger institution) will usually now expect you to submit a *detailed* costing sheet that expands on the rough preliminary budgets discussed at the pre-production meeting (see Chapter 3). The revised costing sheet should include as much near fully costed information as possible, including information about which costumes are to be made and by whom: workroom staff or outworkers. Which will be hired or sourced from direct purchase online or from stores, and how many costume shop/staff hours will be allocated to the building of each costume for each character?

It is useful to bear the following points in mind when you are putting together your detailed costing sheet:

- Which costumes are the most technically difficult to make?
- Does a specific costume have a significant impact on the storytelling of the production and consequently have to include detailing that cannot be altered or approximated?
- Which actors have specific physical attributes (tall, short, large frame, chest or bust, or a disability) that might affect whether their costume has to be built to order?
- Is the costume designed in a color or pattern that will require dyeing or bespoke digital printing?
- Will the materials for the costume be difficult to source? This might include a large number of costumes designed to be identical.
- Will there need to be extra copies of the costume made (called 'doubles') because of special effects or extreme wear and tear in performance, or for understudies?
- If you are working with actors who are of 'high-status' within the industry, you may need to budget for certain sundries, such as underwear, hosiery and footwear, that might be

classed as 'luxury' items. Sometimes, celebrity actors may have specific requirements written into their contracts to cover certain elements of their costume.

- How many understudies are there to costume?

If you have been engaged to work on your particular production in very good time then you may have been researching and making script breakdown documents for several weeks before the first rehearsal. This was the case for Amanda Hambleton when she was working as the costume designer and supervisor for *Cinderella* at Oxford Playhouse. She began working with director Steve Marmion a full eight months before the opening night of the pantomime. Costings and approximate budgets were decided following creative meetings in April 2016. Amanda described her approach to working with the director on her budgets:

> *You need to get in [the director's] head. Be honest about budget as soon as possible and keep having conversations with them. Be practical, and if there is an issue that crops up with something, then be honest about it. . . . They don't need to know everything, every mundane detail, just what is important.*[1]

Lucy Martin also began work on budgets for *The Deep Blue Sea* three months before rehearsals began. The supervisors on *The Man of Mode* were working with an even longer lead time with regard to budget, as the fabrics had to be sourced very early to allow the maximum time for the student costume interpreters to complete the complex, historically accurate 'Restoration'-inspired designs.

CREATING A COSTING SHEET

The costing sheet for *The Deep Blue Sea* (Figure 5.1) demonstrates the elements that would be expected: every component is budgeted for, to complete the designer's requirements. If more information is needed, perhaps because of late casting of an actor, or if the designer or director needs rehearsal time to make a final decision about an element of costume, then an 'educated' estimate is made. The costume supervisor needs to have gathered enough information following production meetings, the first rehearsal read-through and surveys of the costume stock available to decide which costumes are to be made, hired or sourced to be able to commit each and every item to their costing spreadsheet.

It is advisable to include the following primary headings on your spreadsheet (usually created in Excel from the Microsoft Office suite (see Appendix 5 for a simple guide to Excel):

- Performer
- Character/Scene
- Number of Costumes
- Notes (any specific or special requirements)
- Make/Hire/Buy

Show: The Deep Blue Sea
Show Code:
Theatre: Lyttleton

ALLOCATED HOURS	
Workshop hrs	960
Alterations hrs	120
Cost-prop making hrs	200
Tech hrs	100

Performer	Character/ Scene	No of costumes	Notes	Buy, Make, Hire Dpt	Outside Hires £	Outworker £	Materials/ Bought goods £	Workshop Hrs Men's Workroom	Workshop Hrs Women's Workroom	Costume Prop Hrs (IH)
Helen	Hester Collyer - underwear		1940s bra, stockings etc tbc	Buy			120			
McCrory	Hester Collyer - day dress Act 1	1		Make			200			
	Hester Collyer - slip, Act 1		Vintage	Buy			150			
	Hester Collyer - dressing gown Act 1	2	Specific colour, might be dyed	Make			200		40	
	Hester Collyer - outfit 2, Act 2	3	Skirt and jumper - possible	Make			250		100	
	Hester Collyer - coat, Act 2		Possible buy?	Make			200		100	
	Hester Collyer - hat, Act 2		Vintage	Buy			120			
	Hester Collyer - shoes, Act 2			Buy			150			
	Hester Collyer - accessories, jewellery etc		Bracelet, watch - mentioned in script				100			
	VIntage buys / non returnable items			Buy			500			
Tom	Freddie Page - shirts			Buy			140			
Burton	Freddie Page - suit 1	1	Suit or separates	Hire	440					
	Freddie Page - coat & hat			Hire	120					
	Freddie Page - suit 2	2	Blue, colour is important	Make			250	70		
	Freddie Page - shoes		Possibly 2 pairs	Buy			100			
	Freddie Page - vintage & accessories		Ties, watch etc	Buy			100			
Peter	William Collyer - shirts			Buy			140			
Sullivan	William Collyer - suit 1	1	Morning suit	Hire	440					
	William Collyer - coat & hat			Hire	120					
	William Collyer - suit 2	2	TBC - changed from morning suit? * arrives straight from court, keeps coat on?	Hire	440					
	William Collyer - suit 3	3	Dinner suit TBC	Hire	440					
	William Collyer - shoes		2 pairs	NT stock						
	William Collyer - accessories		Vintage	Buy			60			

Figure 5.1 Fragment/screenshot from the costing sheet for *The Deep Blue Sea*

Source: Courtesy of the National Theatre, and created by Lucy Martin in Microsoft Excel.

- Hired Externally (as an outside hire)?
- Made Externally (by an outworker)?

The following categories would only apply if you were working in a large theatre with separate workrooms for female and male costume, costume prop and dye shop:

- workroom hours to make each costume item, divided into male and female;
- costume prop-making hours;
- dye shop hours.

Close inspection of the costing sheet for *The Deep Blue Sea* (see Figure 5.1) reveals that most items for the three actors listed on this sheet were 'buys' – sourced from vintage or contemporary suppliers. There were 'makes' (from the National Theatre costume department) for the lead characters, Hester Collyer and Freddie Page. The notes on the spreadsheet are useful to indicate whether costs are known, fixed and ordered, or speculative. Calculating the time required to make each bespoke costume is an element that will be added to your costing sheet. Tables 5.1 and 5.2 show ready reckoners for calculating costume shop hours for womenswear and menswear respectively. These guides are to be used to begin the process of costing. Working with your production manager or head of costume, the supervisor will have workroom hours approved once the costing sheet projections are made. The tables with estimated hours should be approached with caution, as exact hours will need to be assessed in relation to the detail and complexity of the costume designs.

It is very important to estimate all other fixed costs and extras. With the help of your draper and costume assistant (if you are lucky enough to have one), ascertain exactly what your budget has to cover on top of the in-house workroom hours:

- Are you responsible for wigs and make-up?
- Will costume sourced from theatre stock be charged to your budget?
- Are haberdashery supplies, cotton and threads, calico for toiles (the calico 'mock-up' made for the first fitting) costed through the more general 'costume shop' budget, or your show budgets?
- Are dry cleaning and laundry materials within your budget, or through the running wardrobe costs?
- Is shoe re-soling one of your costs?
- Do you have to account for sourcing prescription spectacles for your actors, or will the production manager deal with this?
- Will you be expected to budget for transport for you, your team and actors to and from fittings if they are rehearsing at a venue that is a distance from your costume shop?
- Do you need to purchase rails and storage solutions for your production?

Finally, you must establish whether the production manager will require you to include sales tax (Value Added Tax in the UK) to the budget. If this be deducted from the final budget

Table 5.1 Womenswear costume hours ready reckoner

	Jacket	Waistcoat	Long Period Skirt	Pants/Trouser	Uniform Jacket	Ladies Coat	Blouse	Corset	Cape	Long Cloak	Pencil Skirt/ A-line Skirt	1950's Cocktail Dress	Contemporary Evening Dress
Pattern	1	1	2	1	3	4	2	3	2	3	2	5	5
Cut	2	1	2	1	2	2	1	2	2	3	1	5	5
Baste	8	4	2	1	3	4	2	2	3	4	1	6	6
Re-cut	3	1	1	1	2	1	1	1	1	2	1	2	2
Make	28	9	8	10	26	26	10	16	12	14	4	30	30
Sub-total	42	17	15	14	36	37	16	24	20	26	9	48	48
Extras/ Braiding	1	1	4	2	8	3	3	2	2	6	1	4	4
Total Inc. Extras	43 hours	18 hours	19 hours	16 hours	44 hours	40 hours	19 hours	26 hours	22 hours	32 increase in hours for hem leveling	10 hours	52 hours	52 hours

	Dressing Gown	Negligee	Generic Petticoat	1880 Bustle Dress	Bustle Cage	1850 Crinoline Dress	Crinoline Cage/ Spanish Farthingale	1775 Sack Back Dress	1580 Elizabethan Court Dress	Medieval Dress	Period Hat	Panto Dame	Fur Stole
Pattern	2	4	1	8	1	8	2	8	8	4	1	8	1
Cut	2	6	1	6	2	6	2	6	8	4	2	6	2
Baste	4	8	4	8	—	8	4	12	16	4	4	8	2
Re-cut	2	2	1	5	—	3	2	5	6	2	1	3	1
Make	10	24	6	40	8	40	16	40	50	16	16	40	5
Sub-total	20	44	13	67	11	65	22	71	88	30	24	65	11
Extras/ Braiding	2	4	2	8/16	—	8/16	8	8/16	10/ 20	8/10	8	8/16	2
Total Inc. Extras	22 hours	48 hours	15 hours	75/83 hours	11 hours	73/ 81 hours	30 hours	79/87 hours	98/108 hours	38/40 hours	32 hours	73/81 hours	13 hours

Table 5.2 Menswear costume hours ready reckoner

	Jacket	Waistcoat	Waistcoat (Shawl Collar)	Pants/Trouser	Uniform Jacket	Jodhpurs	Overcoat	Shirt	Frock Coat	Tail Coat	Short Cloak	Long Cloak	Cassock	Quilted Dressing Gown	Dressing Gown	Doublet	Breeches
Pattern	1	1	1	1	2	1	2	2	3	3	3	4	3	3	2	4	2
Cut	2	1	1	1	2	1	2	2	2	2	2	4	3	3	2	4	1
Baste	8	4	6	6	8	6	8	4	8	8	4	8	10	8	6	8	6
Re-cut	3	1	1	1	3	1	3	1	3	3	4	4	2	3	2	4	1
Make	28	9	14	8	26	10	32	6	36	28	12	18	28	26	14	24–32	9
Sub-total	42	16	23	17	41	19	47	15	52	44	25	38	46	43	26	44–52	19
Extras/ Braiding	0	0	0	2	5	4	2	0	4	2	0	0	0	3	2	8–24	2
Total Inc. Extras	42 hours	16 hours	23 hours	19 hours	46 hours	23 hours	49 hours	15 hours	56 hours	46 hours	25 hours	38 hours	46 hours	46 hours	28 hours	52–76 hours	21 hours
	2-piece Suit	3-piece Suit	3-piece Suit + Coat	3-piece (Frock Coat)	3-piece (Tail Coat)	Doublet + Breeches	Notes:										
Quick Reckoner	61 hours	78/80 hours	129/130 hours	117 hours	107 hours	70–100 hours											

reconciliation ,then you will make considerable savings. Time and again, costume supervisors have slipped up by forgetting to take sales tax into consideration! You must know exactly what you are responsible for before you begin to commit to buying fabrics, good and services.

When you are in a position to know what your fixed costs are, you can subtract these from the budget. Be sure to establish a reasonable working contingency of 10 percent of your total budget for emergences before and during your tech week, or check whether this sum is to be held by the production manager. It is very important not to omit the more challenging costume items on your lists, such period shoes which have to be made to order, or fabrics which you know from experience will be difficult to source or have to be sent out to be embroidered or treated in some way. Trust your instinct about these, and tackle them head-on. When the expensive and awkward items have been allocated a budget, you can begin to estimate a price for each and every costume item on your spreadsheet. Costs will still be fluid at this point as you begin the rehearsal process: be flexible, as much can change up until the last week of rehearsal, and even into the tech week. It is at this time that the R (Resourceful) and O (Organized) of ROCK, discussed in Chapter 1, are useful to remember.

ESTIMATING FABRIC QUANTITIES

You will have to estimate the quantities of fabric (including linings, buttons, zips, busks, fastenings, facings and bias bindings) required for your costume shop to build the costumes. These costs can be added to your budget spreadsheet. The handy yardage/meterage guide in Table 5.3 should help with allocating *approximate* quantities. It is very important to remember that these estimated quantities of fabric may vary dramatically if your designer chooses fabric with a large pattern repeat, or if the design requires a lot of embellishment, such as frills, ruffles or flounces.

Alongside this quick fabric quantity calculator, Table 5.4 shows estimated quantities for period costumes. Again, use these only as estimates and with a strong dose of common sense. You must take account of your designer's drawings, looking out for extra embellishments and period details that may require budgeting for. The size and height of your actor must also be an important consideration, as well as the width of the fabric your designer chooses. It would be advisable to consult with your costume draper about the linings and foundation materials required for building complex period garments, as it can be easy to overlook or underestimate some elements required to achieve the correct silhouette.

Finally, consider the costs for all accessories, including hats, underwear, hosiery, jewellery and footwear, and allocate your budget accordingly. Sometimes, it can be difficult to estimate accessories at this stage, as rehearsals are likely to dictate the requirements of the smaller 'personal' costume elements. The supervisor must also consider understudy costumes at this point, although you will not source these (particularly if you are supervising a contemporary production) until the tech week, because you have to set the main cast costume before you can replicate or purchase for the understudies.

Table 5.3 Estimated/basic yardage/meterage for budgeting and sourcing contemporary costume

Womenswear	45–54in (1.37–1.14m) wide	Menswear	45–54in (1.37–1.14m) wide
Contemporary dress (depending on fullness)	3–5.5yds (2.75–5m)	Contemporary suit	
		Single-breasted	4–5yds (3.75–4.75m)
		Double-breasted	4.5–5.5yds (4.25–5m)
Blouse with long sleeves	3yds (2.75m)	Jacket	3.5yds (3.25m)
Blouse with short sleeves	2.75yds (2.5m)	Pants (UK, trousers)	2.5yds (2.25m)
Tailored jacket	3.75yds (3.5m)	Vest/waistcoat fronts	1.5yds (1.5m)
Tailored skirt	2yds (2m)	Jacket lining	4yds (3.75m)
Pants (UK, trousers)	2.5yds (2.25m)	Shirt	3.25yds (3.25m)
Overcoat	4yds (3.75m)	Overcoat	4.5yds (4.25m)

Notes: These are very rough estimates, and they have been calculated quite generously. You should consider the size of your actor, style of garment and pattern matching of your fabric – e.g. is there a repeat in the fabric that will require extra lengths?

The figures have been rounded up to the next 0.25yds/m, as fabric stores do not usually cut less than 0.25yd/m.

Table 5.4 Estimated yardage/meterage for budgeting and sourcing period costume

Womenswear	45–54in (1.37–1.14m) wide	Menswear	45–54in (1.37–1.14m) wide
Long period skirt (c.1900)	6.5yds (6m)	19th-century morning coat and pants (UK, trousers)	6.5yds (6m)
1880 bustle dress	11–16.5yds (10–12m)	Tailcoat	4.5yds (4.25m)
1850 crinoline dress	11yds (10m)	Breeches (most periods)	2.25yds (2m)
1800 Empire line dress	4.75yds (5m)	18th-century frock coat	6.5–7.75yds (6–7m)
1775 robe anglaise	8.75yds (8m)	18th-century square-cut frock coat (depending on fullness)	7.75yds (7m)
1730 'sack back' dress	13–14.5yds (12–14m)	Period shirt (depending on fullness)	3–4yds (2.75–3.75m)
1680 Restoration dress	11yds (10m)	Trunk hose (16th-century) (depending on fullness)	2.75–3.75yds (3–4m)
1580 Elizabethan court dress	11yds (10m)	Religious cassock (depending on fullness)	5.5–6.5yds (5–7m)
Medieval dress	7.5yds (8m)	Period overcoat	5yds (4.5m)
Bodice and sleeves	3.25yds (3m)	Doublet (16th and 17th-century)	3.25yds (3m)
Corset	1.25–2.25yds (1–2m)	Medieval tunic	3.25yds (3m)

Note: This is a very rough suggestion of quantities when estimating costs for period costume. It may be useful to consider using this formula for calculating fabric quantities for women's skirts: 3 widths of fabric × the waist to ground measurement + 0.25yd (20cm).

Table 5.5 shows a simple reckoner for translating yards, as used in the United States, to meters, which are commonly used in Europe and the United Kingdom. If you are working in Europe, it is a really useful skill if you learn to be 'bi-lingual' with metric and imperial measurements and able to convert between the two. It is remarkable how easy this can be to achieve when you have been on the phone for days organizing deliveries!

Figure 5.2 Handling your swatches and receipts when sourcing

I suggest you photocopy the three documents listed below to keep in your shopping file to refer to when out and about or working at your desk:

- the table of estimated yardage/meterage for budgeting and sourcing fabric for contemporary costume;
- the table of estimated yardage/meterage for budgeting and sourcing fabric for period costume;
- the yards to meters ready reckoner.

Table 5.5 Yards to meters ready reckoner

Yards 1yd = 91cm	Meters 1m = 1.09yds	Yards 1yd = 91cm	Meters 1m = 1.09yds
0.10 (3.6in)	0.09	5yds	4.57m
0.25 (9in)	0.22	5.25	4.80
0.50 (18in)	0.45	5.50	5.02
0.75 (27in)	0.68	5.75	5.25
1yd (36in)	0.91m	6yds	5.49m
1.25	1.14	6.25	5.71
1.50	1.37	6.50	5.94
1.75	1.6	6.75	6.17
2yds	1.83m	7yds	6.40m
2.25	2.05	7.25	6.62
2.50	2.28	7.50	6.85
2.75	2.51	7.75	7.08
3yds	2.74m	8yds	7.32m
3.25	2.97	8.25	7.54
3.50	3.20	8.50	7.77
3.75	3.42	8.75	8.00
4yds	3.66m	9yds	8.23m
4.25	3.88	9.25	8.45
4.50	4.11	9.50	8.68
4.75	4.34	9.75	8.91
		10yds	9.14m

If you format this to A5 (UK standard size) or half letter (US standard size), your file should be easily accessible and transportable when hitting the shops or going online to source your costumes. If you then add this to the measurement comparison sheet in Table 5.6 which details all basic measurements for each actor, you will be absolutely ready to go! These items could just as easily be loaded onto your tablet or phone for a more digital approach, but in my experience, the hard-copy analogue approach sometimes works best, as your paper file does not need to be recharged!

As discussed earlier in this chapter, if you are working at a larger theatre, then your shop hours usually have to be accounted for: the estimated total hours required for the building of each costume that has been designated 'make'. This will then be added to the costing spreadsheet. As with costume materials costings, the complexity of the design and details and final

Table 5.6 Measurement comparison sheet

Production Title:									
Artist									
Height									
Dress size									
Suit size									
Neck size/shirt size									
Chest/bust/bra size									
Nape to waist (back)									
Nape to ground									
Across back									
Waist									
Hip/seat									
Arm length									
Inside leg									
Outside leg/rise*									
Head circumference									
Hat size									
Glove size									
Shoe size									
Additional information or measurements (e.g. allergies/tattoos/actor preferences)									

Note: * = outside leg to ground minus inside leg to ground.

finish of the garment must be considered. Will fabric need to be dyed when in pre-construction, or afterwards if the designer requires that the costume be 'broken down'? Will items need to be sent off-site, for example for embroidery? A costume that had to be pre-dyed, then built, and then broken down and/or embroidered will require quite a lot of organization and planning, as well as a longer lead time to completion.

Once your costing sheet is completed and signed off by the production manager, you will draw up a fabric shopping schedule, dates for hire department sourcing expeditions and a potential time frame for costume fittings with your designer and stage management team. You will have begun the process of deciding what will be built, made or sourced after visiting the costume store, ostensibly to look for rehearsal costumes, but also to see what you might be able to use for your production, saving both time and money. Ask questions about the stock, take photographs to help you remember what is available in the store, and begin to build a file with all your research. This will be the first essential element in the creation of your Costume Bible (see Chapter 6). You will now know whether the show is going to be full of bespoke costume 'builds', or whether they will be largely hired or sourced from online suppliers and high street stores. The majority of productions use a combination of all three.

ACCESSING CASH FOR SHOPPING EXPEDITIONS

Some of your budget will need to be available to you in cash in the form of a 'float', and this will usually be accessed by filling out a cash advance form provided by your organization or production manager. Each institution will have different methods, so the following is an example and guide only.

PROCEDURE TO ACCESS CASH FLOAT

- Print off a 'cash advance' form from your finance department.
- Complete it using the appropriate production budget code (your production manager or head of costume will supply this).
- The form should be signed by the production manager or appropriate theatre staff member who holds the budget.
- Take the form to the finance department to access the money.
- Ask whether there is a secure place at the theatre for keeping money, such as a safe. If not, then place the cash in your work bank account (as discussed in Chapter 4) for access by debit card payments. Some theatres will provide you with a credit card that is pre-loaded with money for use on your production. This is the best option, so do ask whether this can be arranged.

There is usually a limit on the amount most institutions will allow you to access at one time, so you will need to plan this yourself if you are doing the sourcing. If you have a larger team, your deputy or buyer may help you to plan for the logistics of cash flow. Once you have spent the float, you then return the receipts and replenish the cash advance as required.

RECEIPT MANAGEMENT

It is essential that any costume supervisor can reconcile their receipts, and balance the production costs and budgets. Managing receipts can be a complex procedure, particularly if there are multiple buyers or assistants working concurrently. The method of receipt management detailed below is a basic guide. First, buy yourself a large zipped wallet for your receipts with a separate compartment for your cards and the cash itself (Figure 5.3). It is highly advisable not to use the wallet you use for your personal cash and credit cards – for obvious reasons (you just don't want to added hassle of muddling the two!).

The usual procedure for the reconciliation of receipts is as follows:

- Print off a costume receipts claim form from your finance department.
- Number each receipt, staple it to a blank sheet of paper, and photocopy it for your own records. This way, you will have a copy of the receipt number, style number of the

Figure 5.3 The costume supervisor's wallet

Photograph: Margaret Maguire.

garment that you can use for referencing in your Costume Bible, and you will easily be able to retrieve the receipt for a late return.

- Fill in the claim form for each receipt.

As discussed earlier, there will probably be set a limit on the amount you may withdraw from your finance department. For the sake of argument, assume the amount claimed may not exceed $200. If this sum was usual in your theatre and you had taken it out, and you had only spent on goods totaling $195.50, you would have to return receipts for that sum and $4.50 in cash to the finance department.

You would reconcile the $195.50 by:

- returning the signed, original advance claim form and receipts to your finance department;
- emailing and giving a copy to the production manager or senior budget holder/finance department;
- keeping a copy for your own records for use later in the Costume Bible.

The figures then need to be added to your costume Excel spreadsheet (budget tracker) so that you can keep an accurate running total of your spending. It is important to note that your head of department or production manager would need to sanction all larger items of spending before you went ahead with ordering. You should have already ascertained whether your personal expenses for travel are to be included in your costume budget. Do not forget to account for these in your final budget reconciliation.

PURCHASE ORDERS

If you are purchasing larger items that need to be ordered in advance, you will need to raise a purchase order. This is a commercial document that is the official order issued by a buyer to a seller indicating the nature, quantity and agreed prices of goods and services. A purchase order can usually only be used by a company with which your theatre has an account.

Your purchase order details will include:

- supplier contact details;
- items required and hire costs (including sales tax, although this is listed separately from the basic cost);
- any delivery and collection charges;
- the show budget code (from the production manager/costume staff budget holder);
- the agreed delivery dates.

The supplier will usually not supply goods until payment has been received, so you will need to factor time for the finance department to administer your purchase order into the order timeframe. In larger institutions, purchase orders can be managed electronically, and therefore speedily. The cost of goods ordered would then automatically be added to your show budget as part of the finance system. This information should be given to the production manager at each production meeting and be reconciled following the tech week/weeks. If you are worried about the budget at any point, liaise with the production manager or costume head of department. The production manager, designer and director will be more irritated if their costume supervisor keeps problems from them, rather than revealing any mistakes or over spends that may have occurred as they happen.

The next chapter will include information about strategies for approaching the first rehearsal, as well as a description of details of an accurate measuring technique. You will need accurate measurements to begin both sourcing the costumes and populating information in your Costume Bible, which by now you should be starting to create alongside the financial costings.

NOTE

1 Amanda Hambleton, interview and email correspondence with the author, 22 July 2016.

CHAPTER 6

First Rehearsal and Creating the Costume Bible

The rehearsal room is the space where the director and actors will develop the work in full collaboration. As a costume supervisor, you want to have one ear on the rehearsal room throughout the process of sourcing your costumes, as so much can be learnt and observed by prudently dropping into see how things are progressing day by day during this almost sacred time in the creative process.

Before the first rehearsal, you may be required to provide the 'rehearsal costume'. These items are usually selected from stock and then looked after in the rehearsal room by the stage management team. If you are working on a period production like Maria Nicholson, supervisor for *The Man of Mode*, you will need to provide shoes, corsets and practice skirts for the female actors to help them develop and manage accurate movement authentic to the late 1600's period. The male actors also required boots, breeches, elaborate hats and frock coats to work with. Providing suitable practice costume can be as much a health and safety consideration as an artistic one, particularly if the actor is to manage steps and awkward levels on-set. Alternatively, it may be that a wide range of more contemporary but vintage period items are required for actors and the director to experiment with. It is a good idea to be mindful that actors can become quite attached to the rehearsal clothes. It is not unknown for the costume shop to have to make replicas of them in certain instances. Lucy Martin took a time to source a collection of beautiful dressing gowns for the leading actor, Helen McCrory, to experiment with for the first scenes in *The Deep Blue Sea*. A replica dressing gown was then carefully re-created based on one of the vintage originals used in rehearsal. It was dyed and altered following fittings. For many actors, it is not uncommon to provide various options of particular costumes for them to work with and fine-tune to suit their vision for the character. The minute detail of every item of clothing will naturally be scrutinized by your actors, and this process can begin at the first rehearsal, with final decisions about which clothing item to use sometimes not finalized until the end of the tech.

FIRST REHEARSAL

The first rehearsal (or 'meet and greet', as it is described at the National Theatre) would usually occur one or two weeks after you have met with your costume shop team. It may be quite a formal event when everyone is on their best behavior on the first day of work! The actors will usually be asked to sit in a circle while the director presents their 'vision' for the production, followed by the designers (set, costume, lighting and sound). If the production has music, the musical director and choreographer will also introduce themselves and their ideas to the performers and wider creative community. The stage management team will be leading the first rehearsal, giving out contact sheets, explaining the correct protocols in relation to Equity or other union rules and regulations, health and safety information, establishing lines of communication, call times and the rehearsal calendar, and generally disseminating information to everyone. As Laurie Kincman explains so succinctly: 'The stage manager's overarching goal is to keep everyone on the same page – facilitating discoveries in the rehearsal hall and sharing those discoveries with personnel not in attendance at the time.'[1]

It is unusual for the costume supervisor to have to speak to the whole group at the first rehearsal, but it is a good idea to have a plan for what you want to achieve. Listening to the read-through can be very enlightening, as it brings the play you have been costing and planning to life. It is a good idea to begin to develop a rapport with the stage management team, particularly the stage manager and deputy stage manager, who will be arranging for your actors to be released for fittings and will be sending out the rehearsal notes (which will contain a specific section that relates to costume) each evening by email.

Your designer may well require support, as they are often very much 'on show' at the first rehearsal read-through. They will have to manage many different practical elements of the production, including presenting the set model and the costume designs, themselves – all very demanding and stressful! Michael Pavelka describes the multi-tasking situation designers find themselves in: 'Presenting your model and drawings can become a minor production in itself!'[2] Everyone will be asking the designer questions, from the production manager, who will require detailed technical information, to the director, asking about props, levels and doorways, to the stage management requiring reference material for furniture. You may find that costume is not at the top of the designer's list of priorities! However, this will change, so give your designer time and they will soon be seeking you out in the costume shop.

Following the first read-through of the script with the actors, you can now add any new pieces of practical information about the staging of the show that you have missed, noticed or learnt to your costume plot breakdown. Note everything down, either by hand or digitally on your laptop or tablet device. Sometimes it is only when you hear the script read out that you realize there is something you have overlooked – the same might be said for your director, designer or actor. Everyone will be focused on this first day, and this can result in some interesting new information or revelations that you have not been able to prepare for. Remember the R for Resourceful in ROCK!

TAKING ACCURATE MEASUREMENTS, AND ETIQUETTE RULES TO BE OBSERVED WHEN MEASURING ACTORS

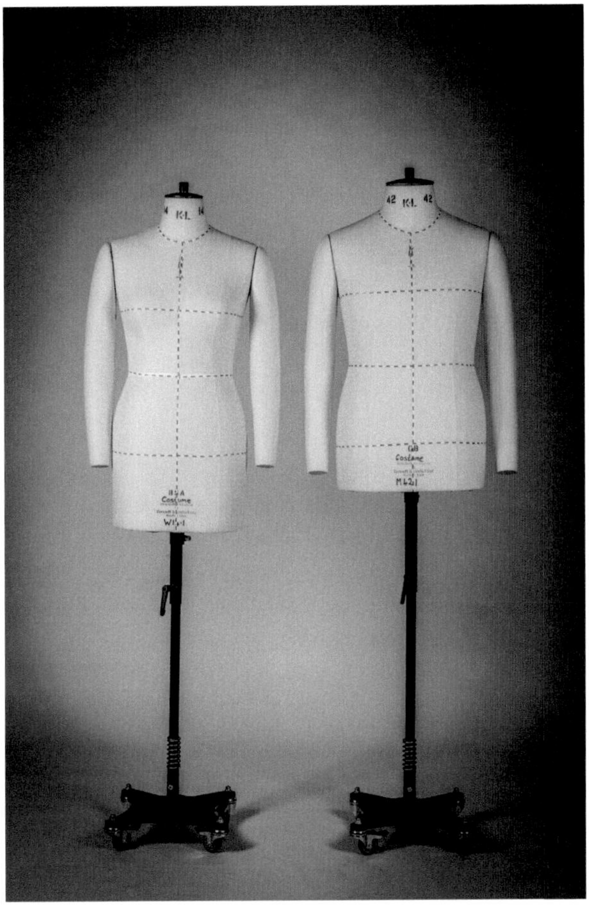

Figure 6.1 Female and male mannequins

Photograph: Margaret Maguire.

It can be customary at the first rehearsal to measure and photograph the actors at some point after the read-through, and this is when you and your assistant or draper can have some time to focus on noting not just practical measurements, but also the personal likes and dislikes of the actors for their costume in performance. Often, actors will confide in the costume supervisor their specific concerns about shoes, underwear, their body shape or how they plan to transform their everyday physicality into their character. Again, this is when the K for Kind in ROCK is important to remember.

Being measured can induce anxiety in an actor, so it is very important to follow a few simple commonsense etiquette rules to help mitigate this. If you are measuring in the rehearsal space on the first day, try to find a convenient and quiet space to work in. It may be a good idea to check the space with your stage management team a few days beforehand, as they will be organizing the space and all the rehearsals. However, quite often, if you are new to the company and freelance, your first rehearsal may be the only time you will have come to the rehearsal room (which is often a rented hall), so it is impossible to plan. You will need a table, one or two chairs, as well of your pre-prepared measurement sheets, a brass-ended tape measure, a 12in metal rule and a notebook and pencil.

It is vital to ensure you take the correct measurements, as they form the foundation of accurate cutting and costume sourcing (see Table 6.1). It is a fact of costume work that everybody will take measurements slightly differently, even following the same method. If at all possible, it is best if the draper can measure the actors with you. Before you begin measuring, ask your draper if they would like to measure in United States Customary System (USCS, known as imperial in the UK, which uses inches etc.), or metric (centimeters). Then discreetly observe the actor being measured: consider the actor's height, build and gait. Do they have any physical characteristics that will affect their costume? This might include postural specifics, such as one shoulder that slopes or a 'long body' in relation to leg length. These notes, recorded at the bottom of the measurement form, will help you to visualize specific details that the simple measurements alone cannot record.

If you are working with actors previously measured by the costume shop, then you only have to check their circumference measures – chest, waist, across back, thigh and neck. Also note that the 'front nape to waist' measurement might be very different if an actor has gained or lost a lot of weight. If you are able to take a full-length photograph of your actor, this will provide you with a great deal of additional information that will support your costume cutting and sourcing. Remember to photograph against a plain white background or wall if possible, and take a headshot and full-length front, back and side views.

In these times of increasing awareness and recognition of gender diversity, it might be interesting, and indeed appropriate, to consider a new approach to the compilation of a set of measurements. The gender-neutral measurement form in Figure 6.2 has been designed to address this issue. Separate male and female measurement forms are also included in Appendix 3 for those who prefer to be gender-specific when working. Once you begin measuring, it is important to note that a small amount of 'ease' should be incorporated into your method of

Table 6.1 Measurements in detail

Make sure that you:
• Conduct the measuring in a private area, especially if clothes have to be removed, and you keep the number of people present to a minimum.
• Have everything you might need at hand (e.g. pencil, measurement sheet and a brass-ended tape measure) before you start, and try to arrange not to be interrupted.
• Ask for any large objects (e.g. keys, wallets) to be removed from pockets, and for any bulky items of clothing to be removed and for your actor to remove their shoes.
• Check with your draper whether they would like the measurements to be recorded in inches or centimeters.
• Familiarize yourself with the sequence of measures to be taken.
• Encourage your actor to stand comfortably and at ease before you start measuring.
• Place a cotton or elastic tape around the actor's waist – this will act as a 'center' to build the measurements from.
• Describe the measurements discreetly in a soft voice to whoever is noting the information for you: working with an assistant or deputy will speed up the process considerably.
• Practice 'safe' measuring methods by standing to the side of the actor, especially for the sensitive measures, e.g. the inside leg and the bust measures.
• Use a brass-ended tape measure that has a rigid end so that actors can position it themselves for the inside leg measurement, avoiding any awkwardness.
• Do not rely on measurements given by an actor or agent without checking them yourself.
• Politely ignore any suggestions of a need for weight loss by the actor, as adjustments can be made at the subsequent fittings.
• *Never* pass comment on any of the measurements or the actor's physical attributes.
• Always take a headshot and full-length photograph of your actor, with a plain background if possible.

measuring. By placing your finger between the body and the tape measure, you will naturally allow for 'ease' (see Figure 6.3).

First, take the actor's height measurement. It is best measured against a wall with your ruler forming a 90-degree angle with the top of the actor's head. While measuring the head, discuss the actor's opinion of their dress/suit and collar size. You can note this at the top of the form. However, it would be a very good idea not to rely on these sizes. Double back after you have

General	**MEASUREMENT FORM**				
	Production		**Date**		**AFFIX ACTOR PHOTO**
	Artist		**Character**		
	Cutter		**Height**		
	Bra Size		**Dress size**		
	Shirt Size		**Suit size**		
	Shoe Size		**Glove size**		
Additional information e.g. Tattoos Allergies					

Head	1. Head Circumference		4. Upper Neck	
	2. Ear to Ear		5. Lower Neck	
	3. Hairline to Nape		Collar	

Major Body	6. Bust/ Chest		8. Waist	
	7.Under Bust		9. Hip/Seat	
Body	10. Waist to Hip/Seat		16. Across Back	
	11. Across Chest		17. Scye depth *1	
	12. Point to Point		18. Nape to Waist (back)	
	13. Nape to Bust Point		19. Nape to Jacket Length (back)	
	14. Nape to under Bust		20. Nape to Knee (back)	
	15. Nape to Waist (front)		21. Nape to Ground (back)	

Arms	22. Shoulder		27. Arm around Bicep	
	23. ½ across Back to Elbow		28. Arm around Elbow	
	24. ½ across Back to Wrist		29. Arm around Forearm	
	25. Arm Length		30. Around Wrist	
	26. Arm around Armhole		31. Around Hand	

Legs	32. Outside Leg to Knee		36. Around Thigh	
	33. Outside Leg to Ground		37. Around Knee	
	34. Inside Leg to Knee		38. Below Knee/'Small'	
	35. Inside leg to Ground		39. Around Calf	
	Rise*2		40. Around Ankle	

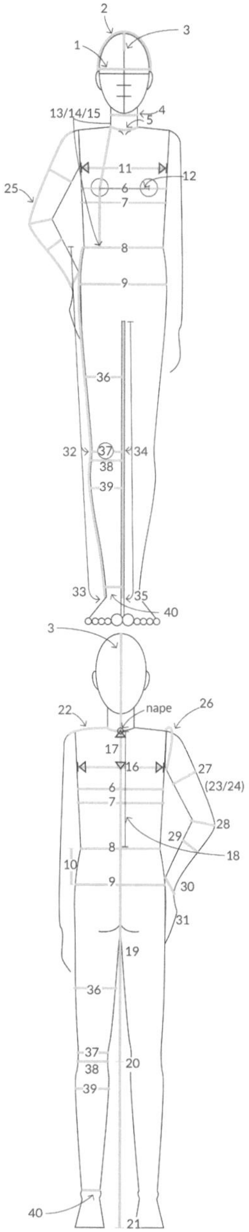

***1 This is a measurement used in tailoring and is the nape to chest line at the back. Measure from the first prominent vertebra at the base of the neck to the back chest/bust line**

***2 Inside leg measurement deducted from outside leg measurement**

Figure 6.2a The gender-neutral measurement form

Source: Designed by Adele Keeley, created in collaboration with Katerina Lawton, Helen Ford and Mandy Barrington.

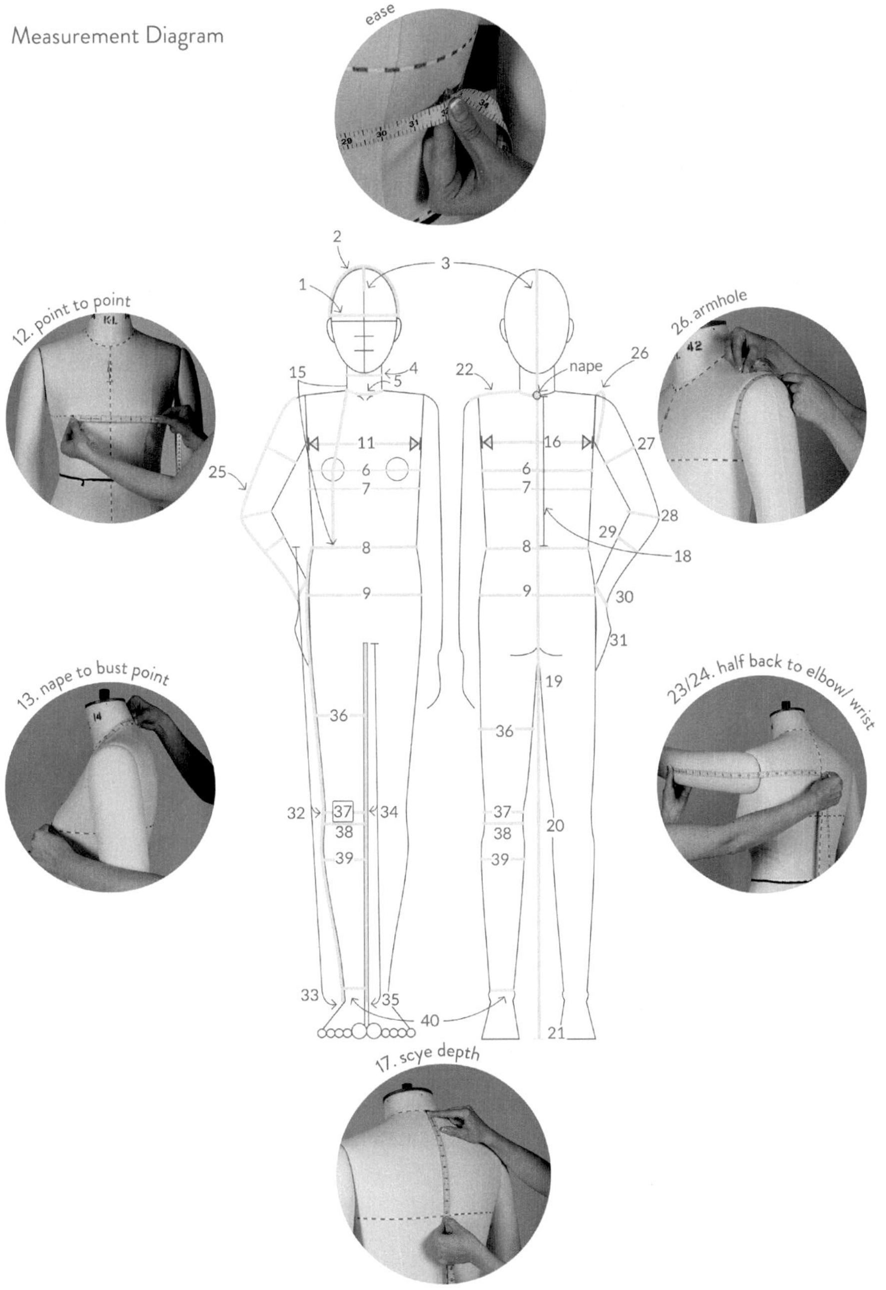

Figure 6.2b (Continued)

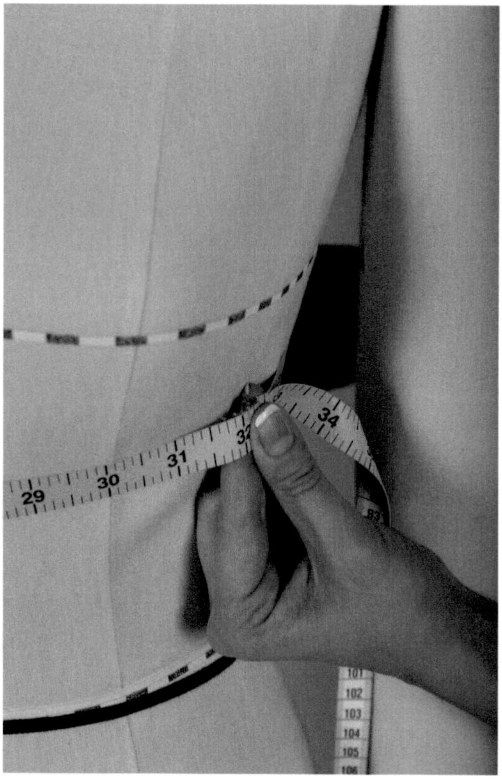

Figure 6.3 Allowing for 'ease' when taking accurate measurements

Photograph: Margaret Maguire.

finished measuring and make you own assessment of the actor's dress or suit size by checking the actual measurements against the proportionate list of standard sizes (proportional measurements in USCS, imperial or metric). It is a great idea to have these charts to hand so you can gauge dress and suit sizes for standard shop-bought items (see Appendix 4 for standard male and female sizing charts).

The correct method of taking each subsequent measure is detailed below. Note that the gender-neutral measurement form is designed with the human body in mind, starting at the head, working down from front to back. A series of numbers can be mapped against the name of each measurement and its corresponding site on the body diagram: HEAD, MAJOR BODY, BODY, ARMS, LEGS.

HEAD

The **head circumference** (labeled '1' in Figure 6.2) measure is taken horizontally from above the ears, around the head, where one might comfortably wear a hat. The **ear to ear** (2) measure is taken from the top of the left ear over the top of the head, to the top of the right ear. The **hairline to nape** (3) measure is taken from the hairline, above the forehead, over the center to the hairline at the base of the neck. The **upper neck** (4) measure is taken 2in (5cm) above lower neck. The **lower neck** (5) is taken at the base of the neck, where it widens. Note that a collar size can be calculated by adding ½in (1cm) to the upper neck measurement. This can be recorded in the 'General' (as the shirt size) and 'Head' sections of the form.

MAJOR BODY

To ascertain the **bust** (female) or **chest** (male) (6) measurement, measure the fullest part around the bust/chest. Be aware that singers and dancers have large lung capacities and that you will need to allow ½ in (1cm) extra 'ease' for this. In opera, it is usual to record both the resting measurement and the singer's exhaling measurement.

The **under bust** (7) measurement is only for women, and should be taken directly under the breasts, around the whole body. The **waist** (8) measurement is taken horizontally right above the hip bones. As mentioned in Table 6.1 above, it can be very useful to fasten a cotton or elastic tape around the waist while taking all measurements. The waist is the smallest part of the body, positioned between the rib cage and the hip bones. If you are having problems identifying where the waist is, ask the actor to put their hands on their hips, when they will usually put them directly on their waist. Note that when discussing the position of the waist line on a costume with the designer and draper, you can adjust the line of the costume to improve the illusion of proportion. The **hip** (female) or **seat** (male) (9) measurement is taken horizontally around the fullest area of the buttocks, measured with the feet together. Beware of any items in pockets. For women, a high hip measurement may also be taken – you should state the distance below the waist at 4in (10cm) and then at 8in (20cm), as this describes the hip area in a little more detail and is useful for a more curvaceous female figure.

BODY

The **waist to hip/seat** (10) measurement is taken from the side of the body, gauging the distance from the waist, to the hip/seat. The **across chest** (11) measurement is taken from the front, measuring the narrowest distance from armhole to armhole above the chest line. The **point to point** (12) measurement, for females only, is taken between the most prominent parts of right and left breast – this is usually between 6in (15cm) and 8in (20cm), but may vary considerably according to breast size. The **nape to bust point** (13) measurement is taken also for females only, from the first prominent vertebra at the top of the center back over the shoulder down to the most prominent part of the bust. This is a very important measurement to ensure that the costume hangs correctly. Then continue to under the bust for the **nape to under bust** (14) measurement. The **nape to waist front** (15) measurement is taken from the first prominent vertebra at the top of the center back over the shoulder down to the most prominent part of the bust and then onto the waist. The **across back** (16) is sometimes called the 'narrow back'. This is measured horizontally above the chest/bust line from the narrowest distance from armhole to armhole. It can be useful to ask your actor to hold a plastic or wooden ruler under each arm so that you can ascertain exactly where the arm meets the body at the armpit.

The **scye depth** (17) is a measurement most commonly used in tailoring, and is the nape to chest line at the back. Measure from the first prominent vertebra at the base of the neck to the back chest/bust line. The **nape to waist back** (18) measurement is taken from the first prominent vertebra at the base of the neck straight down the spine to the waist. Then, from the center back, measure on to the nape to just under buttock line for the **nape to jacket length** (19). This measurement can also be taken as the length from the nape to the point where the actor's thumb extends when resting at their side. Naturally, the jacket length is somewhat arbitrary, as the designer will be deciding this for certain at the fittings, so ask your designer where they will ideally place the jacket hemline. For the **nape to knee** (20) measurement, carry on measuring to the back of the actor's knee. For **nape to ground** (21), measure to the ground.

ARMS

The **shoulder** (22) measurement is taken from the base of the neck towards the arm along to the top of the shoulder joint. The **half across back to elbow** (23) measurement is taken with the arm bent, measuring from spine to elbow along shoulder and arm. For **half across back to wrist** (24), continue measuring to the wrist. To find the sleeve/arm length measurement, deduct half across back from this measurement.

The **arm around armhole** (26) measurement is taken around the circumference of the arm joint from the very top of the arm over the shoulder and under the arm, then back to meet the top again. The **arm around bicep** (27) measurement is the circumference taken at the widest point of the upper arm, usually with the arm bent so that the muscle is extended to its widest point. The **arm around elbow** (28) measurement is the circumference taken at the widest point of the elbow joint, also with the arm bent. For **arm around forearm** (29), measure the fullest part of the forearm, below the elbow. For **around wrist** (30), measure around the wrist, including the bony joint. For **around hand** (31), measure around the palm of the hand, with the hand held flat and the fingers together, missing out the thumb. For your actor's glove size, measure (in inches) around the dominant hand, at the point where the fingers join the hand itself (just below the knuckles – see Appendix 4 for a glove size chart). Record this on the general section of the form.

LEGS

The **outside leg to knee** (32) measurement is taken from the waist level along the side seam to the knee. The **outside leg to ground** (33) measurement continues the outside leg to knee measurement to the ground. The **inside leg to knee** (34) measurement can be a tricky one to gauge, and requires a sensitive approach. Use a 2in (5cm) brass-ended tape measure and stand to the right-hand side of your actor, ask the actor to place the brass end of the tape measure to the top end of their inside leg seam, and with your right hand take the front measure down to the knee. For the **inside leg to ground** (35) measurement, take the tape measure onto the ground. To calculate the **rise**, deduct the inside leg measurement from outside leg measurement. The inside leg measurements ought only to be taken if the actor is wearing pants/trousers. The rise can be measured without recourse to a calculation. Sit your actor on a table or chair, and measure from the waist along the side seam to the top of chair/table – this measurement should be approximately the same as the inside leg measurement deducted from the outside leg measurement.

The **around thigh** (36) measurement is taken as the circumference of the fullest part of the thigh. Beware of differently developed legs: one side might be bigger than the other, so always choose the larger for your final measurement. Ask your actor if they do a lot of sports that might develop one leg over the other. The **around knee** (37) measurement is taken around the widest part of the straight knee. Then measure directly below the knee for the **below knee** (38), sometimes known as 'the small'. The **around calf** (39) measurement is the circumference of the fullest part of the calf. The **around ankle** (40) measurement is taken around the narrowest part of the ankle. Another measurement you may require is the **girth**. There are two ways to measure girth: 'long' and 'short'. The first involves measuring the distance from the center front waist to the center back waist through the legs, which equals the **short girth**, and then from the front nape to the back nape through the legs, which equals the **long girth**. These measurements are a useful control measure when making tight-fitting garments such as leotards or dancewear.

Once you have all your measurements and are back in the costume shop, you can add the measurements for the whole cast to your comparison sheet (see Table 5.6) or 'cheat sheet' and then place the sheets themselves in your new Costume Bible. The comparison chart will be the most essential document when on shopping or sourcing expeditions.

RECORDING INFORMATION IN THE COSTUME BIBLE

The Costume Bible is a simple file that must contain *all* the information related to the costumes in the production. It is the analogue method that supervisors use to communicate every detail to anybody who might be asked to restage the show in the future. The file is usually handed over to the running wardrobe team on the first night, following previews, and may be one of the only written artefacts that survives following the final performance, and as such is a very precious document. This is a fact that museums and theatre archives are now becoming more and more aware of. The National Theatre Archive in London (see Useful Addresses) has a Costume Bible from every production ever staged since its inaugural production of *Hamlet* in 1963, and it is a very interesting resource for any student costume supervisor or researcher.

In the UK, the Costume Bible is typically A4 size. Paper sizes vary between the UK and USA, but for the sake of simplicity, I will refer to the standard UK A4 size (which is approximately the equivalent of US letter size). The main sheet you will need to begin compiling your Costume Bible is the Costume Bible template sheet (Table 6.2).

Table 6.2 Costume Bible template sheet

Production:		1st Rehearsal	
Designer:		1st Onstage	
Supervisor:		1st Preview:	
Maker:		1st Night:	
Artist:			
Character:			
Costume, Scene e.g. Dame Ball, dress, Act 3, Sc. 3	Supplier, Size, Price, Reference Number or Hire Details	Quantity	Fabric Sample/ Barcode
	• List of each item sourced, e.g. boots/socks, underwear, with the corresponding cost		• List of every fabric and which supplier and quantities, with the corresponding sample, cost and barcode • List of all items, with treatments, e.g. dye room
	• List of which costumes are hired and which are made, with details of which hire company, including theatre stock		
	• It can be useful to color-code which items are made, hired or sourced		

Figures 6.4–6.8 indicate each of the stages of the record for one character as they may appear in the file: in this case, for Mr Medley from *The Man of Mode*, designed by Emily Turner and supervised by Maria Nicholson. Some supervisors may vary the way they present their Costume Bibles, but Table 6.3 lists a logical sequence for the necessary information.

It is undoubtedly a relatively straightforward, if time-consuming, task to create your Costume Bible digitally using a laptop, but it needs to be consistently managed throughout

Figure 6.4 The first typical Costume Bible page from *The Man of Mode*: mood board and costume design

Source: Created by Maria Nicholson, costumes designed by Emily Turner. Photograph by Margaret Maguire.

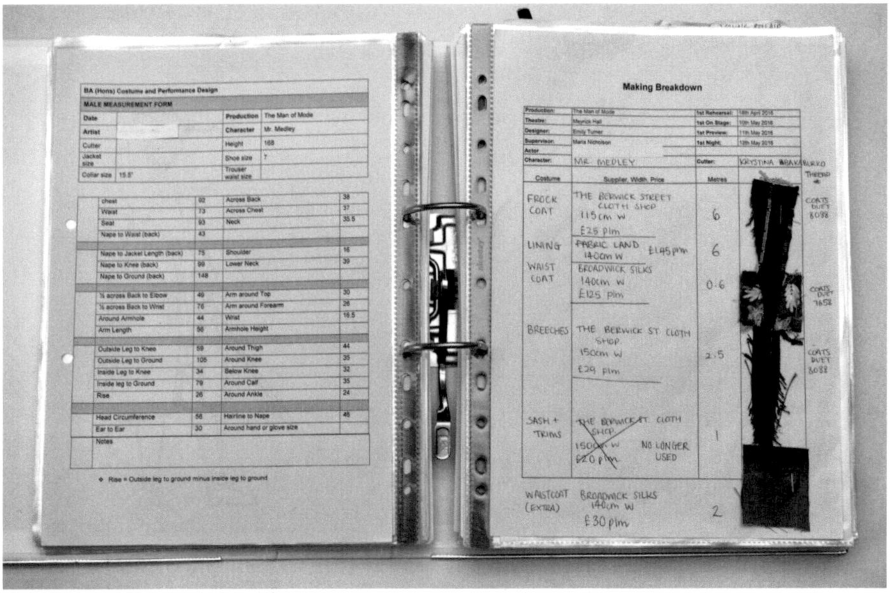

Figure 6.5 The second typical Costume Bible page from *The Man of Mode*: measurement form and making breakdown sheet

Source: Created by Maria Nicholson, photograph by Margaret Maguire.

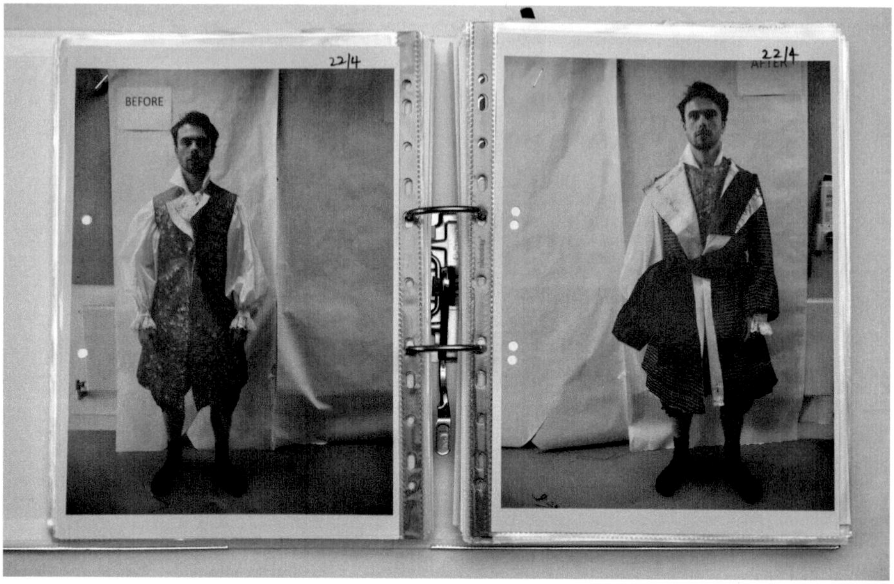

Figure 6.6 The third typical Costume Bible page from *The Man of Mode*: before and after fitting images

Source: Created by Maria Nicholson, photograph by Margaret Maguire.

Figure 6.7 The fourth typical Costume Bible page from *The Man of Mode*: the finished costume, front, back and side views

Source: Created by Maria Nicholson, photograph by Margaret Maguire.

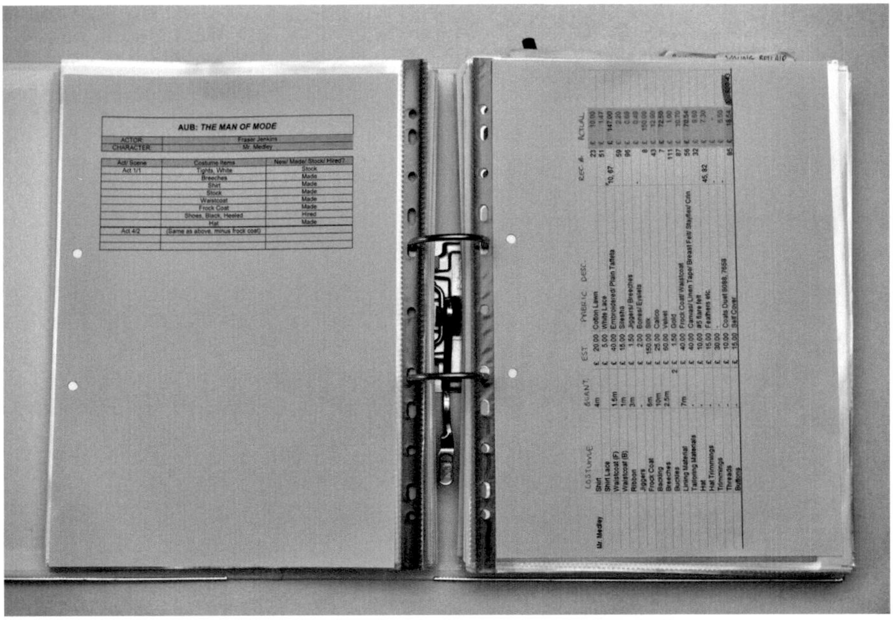

Figure 6.8 The fifth typical Costume Bible page from *The Man of Mode*: costume description list and budget sheet

Source: Created by Maria Nicholson, photograph by Margaret Maguire.

the rehearsal and costume sourcing period, as information can easily be lost or forgotten. Chapter 7 will focus on managing the sourcing of costumes in relation to making, shopping and hiring. Preparation for the first fitting will now be in full swing, with appointments scheduled with the stage management team and the actors. You will by now have allocated costumes to your costume team or to freelancer makers. You may even be making some of the costumes yourself (if you are working for a smaller company or theatre). Your relationship with your designer should be developing, as you have been so busy working together up to this point. If you are collaborating with an experienced designer, then they may be leaving you to your own devices to source fabrics and haberdashery, or you may be working with a novice designer who wants to accompany you on every shopping expedition. Either way, time will now be flying by at an alarming rate.

Table 6.3 The Costume Bible checklist

The Costume Bible should include a section for each character in your production, with a copy of:
1. the contact sheet for the creative team, cast and crew
2. each costume design or the visual reference provided by the costume designer
3. a measurement sheet for each actor
4. a photograph of each actor – a headshot and full-length shot – as well as a record of any fitting images
5. the detailed Costume Bible sheets, including:
6. a breakdown, with swatches, of all the fabrics/trims used in each costume and which supplier they were sourced from, as well as the width, length, quantity and price
7. details of hired costumes, including a breakdown of all the hired items sourced for each character and which supplier they were sourced from, along with the company name, booking out number, appropriate codes, condition and descriptions and descriptions of the work needed to do for the 'return' of the costume to the rental/hire company
8. details of sourced or bought costumes/items, including the store name, product code, the cost and size that was purchased; in an ideal world, the Costume Bible sheet will include the clothing tag, but photographs can be used to record any fabrics or sourced (bought) costume items that don't have a product code or tag (because the item is vintage, or the sources/supplier details have been lost)
9. a record of any treatment (e.g. dyes, print, breaking down) for each costume element
10. an image of the finished costume on either the actor or a dress form
11. your costume plots and breakdown plans
12. the full set of rehearsal notes and tech week notes
13. all information relating to finances and the budget, with the final reconciled accounts for your production

NOTES

1 Laurie Kincman, *The Stage Manager's Toolkit* (New York: Focal Press, 2013), 83.

2 Michael Pavelka, *So You Want to Be a Theatre Designer?* (London: Nick Hern Books, 2015), 256.

CHAPTER 7

Sourcing: Construct, Hire or Buy?

Combining bespoke makes, hires and sourced costumes so that they blend seamlessly as a coherent whole, reflecting the designer's design, is a key skill for any supervisor. It can feel as much like a giant puzzle to get to the final complete rail of costumes, and much will rely on the supervisor's instinct and judgment, as well as a modicum of luck when fabric sourcing, hiring and shopping.

At the National Theatre, 'Costume Chats' are routinely organized so that the director, designer and supervisor can meet with the actors individually to discuss how their feeling for the character they embody connects with the intended costume. This meeting will naturally be scheduled at the beginning of the rehearsal process. This is an example of really good practice, as it is a powerful gesture that recognizes the vital importance of costume in theatre-making. Lucy Martin, supervisor for *The Deep Blue Sea*, described how the National Theatre: 'Costume Chat' tradition was:

> *a very helpful process; a time to 'read' the actor and consequently learn to understand and discuss their individual creative impetus for their role. I can learn what is important to them from a costume point of view. The meeting is 20 or 30 minutes and it is a chance for the costume supervisor to listen to all the creative ideas in one place.*[1]

A costume that is made as a bespoke item is in some ways the easiest to achieve because the designer and costume team can control every aspect of construction and fit, although it will involve a lot of planning and probably be costlier to achieve than a hire. The supervisor must source the correct fabrics either before or while the draper cuts the pattern and creates the initial toile for the performer. It can be a frustrating experience to find the perfect color match and weight of fabric to complement the designs you are interpreting. Some designers accompany you or the buyer (if you have one) on shopping expeditions. Alternatively, some designers may prefer to choose fabrics from samples that have been sourced for them by the supervisor or buyers either from stock or from sample books in the workroom. Fabrics may also be ordered online. It is important to order or purchase more fabric that you think you might need, because changes and adjustments always happen and it can be expensive and creatively disappointing if an inadequate amount of fabric is purchased. This unfortunate situation occurred on *The Man of Mode*. As explained in earlier chapters, the play concerns the habits and lifestyle of the wealthy in Restoration London in the 1660's, so the clothing had to exude a sense of luxury and indulgence. This was a significant aspect of the storytelling, as the title of the play clearly suggests. The designer and the costume supervisor were also working with a very specific color scheme, and it was decided that silks and natural fabrics were ideal to further signify the period of the piece. Obviously, natural fabrics – silks, linens and rich cottons – are expensive, so the supervisor was understandably careful to buy only what was needed, following the toile stage of cutting. However, there were several issues during the fittings which necessitated re-cutting of some pieces, notably an embroidered green waistcoat for Mr Medley, one of the more flamboyant characters. The supplier had no more of the original fabric, so side panels of plain green dupion had to be added, with the silk used only for the centre front. The lustrous green embroidered fabric can be seen quite clearly in Figure 7.1 from a sourcing expedition to Berwick Street in the London theatre district (Figure 7.2).

Berwick Street has many good-quality fabric shops such as Cloth House, Broadwick Silks, Soho Silks and Borovicks. These shops supply some of the biggest costume departments and theatres in the UK, but they can be fairly intimidating places for a novice buyer, supervisor or

Figure 7.1 Shopping for *The Man of Mode* on Berwick Street

Photograph: Margaret Maguire.

Figure 7.2
Haberdashery shopping on Berwick Street

Photograph: Margaret Maguire.

designer. However, when sourcing fabrics, it is helpful to try to get to know the shop assistants. Be friendly and chat to them so that they remember you. This way, they will go out of their way to help you find the exact fabric you need. Remember that they have a huge amount of knowledge about the fabrics they stock and are creative people themselves, so make them part of your process too. One supervisor, when discussing the art of shopping, explained how sourcing fabric for a show is: 'all about legwork and accurate shopping lists. I tend to be careful about the Internet because fabrics are tactile. Shopping for fabrics should be a hugely creative process.'[2] When sourcing with the designer Emily Turner, the supervisor Maria Nicholson first visited the fabric shops to find suitable fabrics, asked for swatches, and then took an hour to discuss which to finally select for purchase. It is very important to allow your designer to feel that they are fully engaged in the discussion process, so a convivial coffee or lunch break when on sourcing expeditions is always a good idea, to allow time to debate choices, then make decisions about any changes and calculate fabric costs. As Nicholson explains: 'You need to think on your feet and always have a Plan B.'[3]

On the periphery of London, Shepherd's Bush (Goldhawk Road tube station) has a good range of fabric shops, which are much cheaper than those on Berwick Street. The eagle-eyed supervisor can often find an identical or very similar fabric for a much better price.

Ideally, you will want to take color copies of the designs with you when you go shopping. File them in a presentation folder that is easily accessible. This will help you to source more accurately, and you will also find that shops are much more willing to help you if they can see the designs and then discuss the sort of fabric you are after and its purpose. A carefully organized file will show that you are a serious and professional supervisor. Remember the O for Organized in ROCK!

Many shops do not like to give samples. If you are working for a recognized theatre, then mention it. Be prepared to buy ¼yd (25cm) of fabric as a sample, as this will really help you in the long run when you go back to the costume shop to discuss with your designer and team which fabrics to choose. Buying samples should never be seen as a waste of money. Budget for it. It is helpful to bring back quite a range of fabrics for the designer to choose from. You will want to make sure you record the price, width, identification number and which supplier they came from on all your samples. It is a good idea to check how much fabric is in stock and whether more can be ordered before you offer it up to your designer, for the reasons mentioned above.

It is important to think very carefully about fabric, not only the color and type, but also, the weight of it and how it will need to be used. A good supervisor, like a great designer, learns to develop fabric sense: the ability to understand the intrinsic properties of fabric, its durability and what qualities it can communicate to the audience. Pamela Howard describes the vital importance of choosing the correct weight costume: 'If the fabric is wrongly "cast" at the decision-making stage, it will never be right for the part. No amount of work will make a fabric behave in a manner of which it is incapable.'[4]

Getting the right color and shade of fabric can be very important, and a matter of principle for designers. The designer is trying to make a strong connection between the colors in their costume drawing or research material and the final realized costume. This can be difficult for the supervisor to negotiate and support if that particular hue of lilac satin (or whatever it is) simply cannot be found in the correct quantity or weight. The designer will also be very particular about color because they are acutely aware that all the fabrics need to sit well together visually onstage. Remember that some fabrics can be dyed to order, or just 'dipped' to alter the color slightly. The dye process is not suitable for some synthetic fabrics or fabrics that are too delicate. A conversation with and sampling by the dye room team, if you have one, will help you to decide whether a fabric will be adversely affected by the dyeing process and the texture and weight compromised. However, color is irrelevant if the weight of the fabric is wrong. As a supervisor, you have to balance all the requirements of the design and making to create a great costume with the correct aesthetic and durability.

You must also be able to calculate the amount of fabric that will be needed for each costume (see Tables 5.3 and 5.4 for estimated yardage/meterage for budgeting and sourcing for contemporary and period costumes respectively). Don't forget to take the width into account. Sometimes it is good to take a chance on an instinctive feeling with a fabric. If you think it's right, then sample it and show it to the designer. It might not be exactly what they had in mind, but they may prefer it if the fabric is there in the flesh in the workroom. Sample books can also provide you with a quick way to shop for fabrics. Large companies like the National Theatre, have an in-house pattern room that holds sample books of the most up-to-date fabrics from all suppliers. Online sources can also provide swatches if you are working in a smaller theatre or costume shop.

It is very important to remember that you also need to source all the haberdashery items, linings, trimmings and costume sundries in good time. This can be a challenge to manage when you have your draper and stitchers working busily, as you really cannot afford to hold them up. Some designers like to choose all their own notions (fabric trims and buttons), and some even like to choose their own threads, so you can see that an enormous amount of planning is required to co-ordinate the availability of the designer for sourcing so that your stitchers are not held up. It can often take just as long to complete the purchase of all the haberdashery items as to buy the main fabrics. Layering trims and choosing buttons and linings can involves hours of legwork, as in my experience, for some reason, there is never enough of the exact trim you want or large enough quantities of those perfect gold buttons your designer loved so much!

COSTUME HIRE STORES

In London, you can find an extensive range of good costume hire companies, including Angels, Cosprop and the National Theatre (Figure 7.3). In the provinces, the Royal Shakespeare Company, Bristol Costume Services and Birmingham Costume Hire also hold extensive stock. Hiring costumes will probably be much cheaper than making bespoke ones, but costs for hires

Figure 7.3 The National Theatre Hire Department at The Oval, London

Photograph: Courtesy of the National Theatre.

can really add up, so you should do your homework with regard to budget before you book an appointment to go and see them. In the USA (perhaps because of the size of the country), costumes can often be booked online from hire companies and delivered to your theatre, although this is a less common practice in the UK. Western Costume (located in Los Angeles) is the main costume supplier and is the first port of call in the USA. As Nancy Hills explained to me: 'Everything is shipped around the States online. I can't imagine how we did anything before the Internet!'[5]

Receiving pre-ordered costumes is convenient, but there is great joy to be found hunting in person for costumes in hire companies. It can feel like a monumental task at first, like a giant game of chess, but with preparation, it can save you a lot of time and money. Be careful to scrutinize the costume designs again before you book your visit to a hire house. Look out for shapes and silhouettes, and organize your list of desirables so that the awkward items are at the top of the list for consideration first. When you arrive, you will often be assigned a costumier who will assist you. The costumier will help you to select costumes and fit them, and will then prepare them for collection. The amount of involvement varies in each costume house, so it is always best to check how things are done when you arrive. Costumiers can often save your skin in the worst situations, so remember this and try to develop a good working relationship with them right from your first visit. Be careful with their stock: ask their permission before you attack the rails, and it is best to show them that you will respect their knowledge of the stock. The costumier will also manage the paperwork for your eventual hire, negotiating the cost, so developing a good working relationship may end up saving your budget too. Costs for hired costumes work on weekly terms that reduce after the first week of hire, on a sliding scale. The shorter the run, the proportionally higher the cost per week – for example, first week £1,000, second week £750, third week £500, and that final sum for all subsequent weeks

The process of selecting from hired stock is called 'pulling'. When pulling costumes for a production, you should start by looking for a range of sizes and an overall color theme that allows many combinations to work. As one supervisor explained:

> *When hiring, you select first and pull a rail together and then take the designer to see what you have found that fits with their design, fits the actor (hopefully) and is not too worn. You can then go back through the rails with the designer and fill the gaps.*[6]

If you are a very experienced supervisor, you will have developed an extensive knowledge of the costume stock available from a specific hire company. You may consider whether costumes can be created partly from an existing garment with bespoke elements sourced, or made to enhance and personalize them in line with the designer's original drawings or research materials – this is when the C for Creative in ROCK comes into play. Repurposing existing costume items from either hire or theatre stock (Figure 7.4) can be rewarding, as well as cost-effective and ecologically sensible. There is often something intangible but wonderful about a costume that has been added to carefully and creatively. It is almost as if the costume and the aura of the previous production it was originally made for is preserved and contributes to the energy of the new production. It can produce a sort of costume alchemy. The skill here for

Figure 7.4 The Costume Store at the Arts University Bournemouth

Photograph: Margaret Maguire.

the supervisor is all about 'blending' the found items with the makes, hires and shop-bought items to create something fresh and original. A common scenario might be like this: we are planning to make that black bustle skirt circa 1885 from that particular fabric because Actor A is very tall, so will the bodice we know would work (and fit) from our favorite hire company work with the bespoke skirt? Our actor is very slender and her arms are long, so will the hire company allow us to add lace to the cuffs to mitigate for this? This is before we even know whether the bodice is available for the run of the production. All these questions are running through your mind if you are visiting a hire store.

If you are looking through the theatre's own stock, the costume can often be altered or even dyed to work for the production. If you are hiring from an outside hire company, then any changes you wish to make must be discussed with the hire company costumiers, just as any changes *must* be reinstated before the return. Often, substantial alterations will not be possible. Damage to costumes will be charged on return by the hire company or taken from the deposit.

You will often put costumes together working from your actors' measurements without a fitting, so select costumes with a good seam allowance (these are sometimes called 'inlays'). The seam allowance is the area between the edge of the garment piece and the stitching line, and can vary from ¼in (6mm) to several inches, so a standard amount cannot be taken for granted. A good seam allowance will allow you to potentially 'let out' or 'take in' costumes to improve fit. If you are working for a student production or a smaller-scale theatre, you may not be able to afford the large hire companies for all the characters, so you may choose to focus your time and budget on only hiring for the principals. Most regions have costume hire companies, and although some of the selections may not be as good, the cost is usually much less, and if you really rummage through the rails, you will often be surprised what you can find.

SHOPPING

On a large production, there may be multiple buyers responsible for different areas of the show, and the costume supervisor acts as a veritable 'air traffic controller', sending out the buyers with epic shopping lists and numerous returns of shop-bought items following fittings. On a smaller production, the role of costume supervisor and buyer will usually be combined. Creating exact and detailed shopping lists is a real skill that develops naturally with experience. A quick meeting with your buyers in the morning before you shop should help you to focus and describe what you need sourced and from where.

The longer you work as a supervisor, the easier it will become to know where to source goods and materials. If you are looking for something unusual, then be imaginative about where you look. The Internet is a great resource these days, and websites like eBay and Etsy can be really helpful for that unusual purchase or vintage item (Figure 7.5). However, it can be very frustrating when deliveries do not arrive on time, so you should make sure you order Internet-sourced items at the beginning of the rehearsal process, and not just before your technical week, if you possibly can. Shopping for regular clothes in stores has parallels with sourcing costumes in hire stores. You need to focus on finding items based on the complexity of the costume and the awkwardness of sourcing it first – finding the large shoe, the unusual rare vintage item or fabric. Also consider quantities. If you will need 20 pairs of specialist stockings, then it is probably a good idea to order them online, but finding a dress in a specific color will require shopping because you need to see the weight, size and cut of the garment to make an informed decision about its suitability. One supervisor explained that it was their job to make sure a hired or bought costume was 'grounded'. It can be a problem to know this if the correct amount of legwork (that word again) has not been undertaken. Many of the supervisors I spoke to felt a degree of guilt if they relied too heavily on the Internet, even though they acknowledged that they do need to use it. The unreliability of Internet deliveries can be a problem, but this situation will inevitably improve in the future.

Figure 7.5 Beautiful vintage fabrics

Photograph: Margaret Maguire.

It is very important to track your Internet shopping and manage receipts carefully, as the costs can run away with themselves! A centrally managed finance system will mitigate this, but if you are working in a smaller institution, then you will need to add your Internet purchases daily to your budget spreadsheet. It can also be difficult to manage deadlines for items you may wish to return if the costume items are unsuitable following fittings. Adding a column with return date deadlines will help with this perennial issue. One other tip: keep all your packaging from Internet purchases.

NOTES

1 Lucy Martin, interview with the author at the National Theatre, April 2016.
2 Ibid.
3 Maria Nicholson, interview and email correspondence with the author, 15 July 2016.
4 Pamela Howard, *What is Scenography?* (2nd ed., New York: Routledge, 2009), 167.
5 Nancy Hills, interview with the author at the Arts University Bournemouth, June 2016.
6 Lucy Martin, interview with the author at the National Theatre, April 2016.

CHAPTER 8

Managing the Rehearsal Process

FITTINGS

As the rehearsals progress towards the second week, it may well be time for the 'first fitting'. At this crucial time, the company of actors and creatives will be very keen to see whether the costumes that are beginning to emerge from the costume shop work with the staging and imagery that is being created in the rehearsal room. Is everyone on the same page with this show? Rehearsal notes will have been filtered through to the costume supervisor from the stage management team from day one at the 'meet and greet', so by the second week, there should be few surprises in store for the costume shop. It is very important for the supervisor to check the rehearsal notes on a daily basis, as it can be very costly and time-consuming to alter significant costume items as it gets closer and closer to tech week.

The fitting of a costume is a highly creative moment for the designer, but also for the supervisor. It is where the costume designs and reference material can come to life. It is useful to think of both the designer and supervisor 'drawing' the costumes *together* in the fitting room. As Michael Roff explains: 'A fitting is always designer-led, but the actor and the supervisor are equally invested in the process. It is collaborative, or should be.'[1] Fitting a costume should be a *dynamic* and *interactive event*. The fitting room should always be seen as a creative space where the designer, supervisor, draper, actor, and occasionally director, can explore and refine their respective thoughts about the costume in performance. Pamela Howard describes how: 'Tact and psychology, coupled with an understanding of the character to be played, have to be the languages of the fitting room, with a quiet and authoritative calm established.'[2]

The costume supervisor will need to remain calm and focused when the first fittings begin, as occasionally this stage can be quite a daunting experience for actor and designer. It is important that enough time is allocated to each actor when negotiating the schedule for fittings with the deputy stage manager. As a rule, half an hour per costume is ideal. The schedule with timings for the fittings is then distributed by the stage management team to the actors a few days beforehand.

CREATING A CALM FITTING SPACE

The fitting room should be carefully prepared before the fitting, with a large, clean mirror, chairs and a table. There will be a rail, of course. It is important to make sure the room is airy and well ventilated, as actors can be prone to fainting, especially if they are corseted or wearing very heavy uniforms or coats and standing still for a prolonged period of time in a hot environment. Jugs or bottles of water (to prevent dehydration) and perhaps grapes and something sweet to eat (to prevent glycemic dips) are useful additions to any fitting space – just be careful not to damage the costumes with food and drink!

In some workroom fitting spaces, an area will be screened off in order to maintain the privacy of the actor when undressing, although in others, like the National Theatre, actors dress in the open room with the supervisor or their deputy assisting (Figure 8.1). It is very useful if the deputy can then manage writing up the to-do list, as juggling actor, costume and list may challenge even the most experienced supervisor. The draper will usually also be on hand to advise and assist in the process of fitting the costume itself.

It is essential that the supervisor has prepared a basic fitting room kit (Figure 8.2) prior to the beginning of the session, including the following items:

- a notebook and pencil;
- tailor's chalk and invisible marker;
- small, sharp scissors for cutting into seams if required;
- larger shears in case you need to cut a large amount of fabric;
- a variety of machine seam cutting tools (un-pickers);
- pins in all sizes, plus a pin cushion of your choice;
- safety pins in all sizes;
- a clothes brush and lint roller;
- cotton tape;
- a tape measure;

Figure 8.1 A fitting room at the National Theatre

Photograph: Courtesy of the National Theatre.

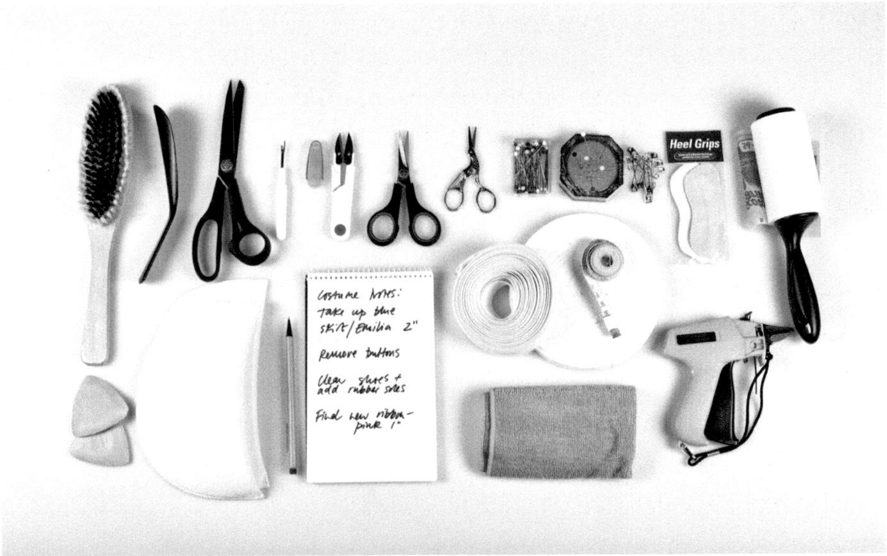

Figure 8.2 Fitting room kit

Photograph: Margaret Maguire.

- shoulder pads/insoles/elastic/calico;
- a shop tag gun for quick hemming;
- micro-fiber cloths for cleaning;
- a shoe horn;
- heel grips.

A digital camera will also be an essential item for your fitting kit list, as 'before' and 'after' photographs are a necessary element to be added to the Costume Bible. A cell phone may suffice for this purpose, but make sure it is fully charged before you begin. Some costume supervisors prefer to wear the newer multipurpose costumier belts that can hold all manner of items so they are ready for anything (see Figure 8.3). Time is precious, so these accessories keep everything to hand and less time is wasted. From the outset of the fitting, the costume supervisor will have also prepared or sourced the underwear, tights and shoes (or approximations) for each costume. Judging the creative aspects or practical elements of a costume is impossible without determining the correct foundations or underpinnings, so these elements must be discussed with the designer and draper, and then decided upon and sourced prior to the fitting process.

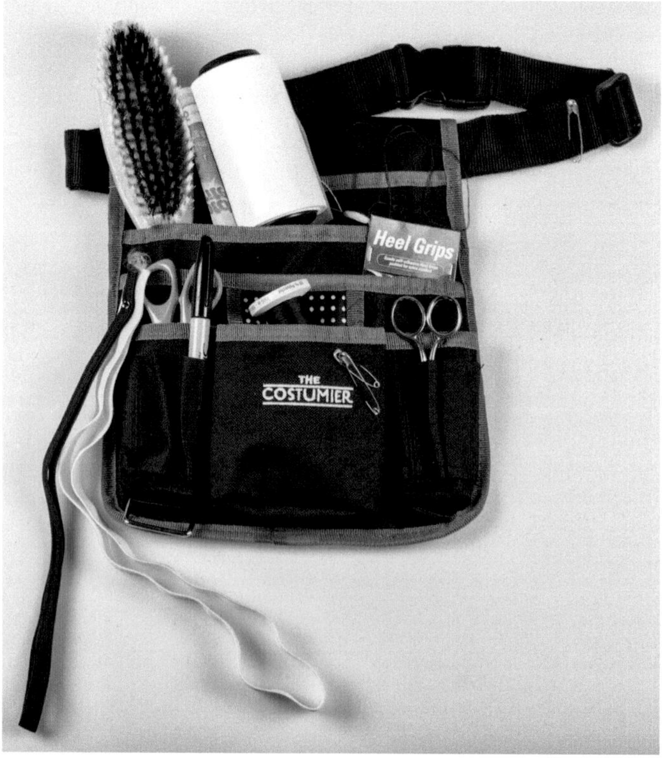

Figure 8.3 Fitting room 'costumier' belt

Photograph: Margaret Maguire.

If the first fitting will only be a 'toile fitting' (Figure 8.4), then the calico costume should ideally be prepared by pressing it beforehand. It is usual for the costume team or possibly dye room team to have created textile samples to consider alongside the toile. Naturally, the designer will be principally concerned with the overall line, silhouette and look of the costume and the connection between all these elements and the embodiment of the visual storytelling. The draper will be focused on the practicalities of fit. The director may be worrying whether the actor can move easily or perform all the actions that have been meticulously rehearsed that week. The actors themselves may worry about how they look physically and whether the image in the mirror connects visually with their impression of the character. Does this costume actually help them achieve their vision for the role? The supervisor will be looking at *every* aspect of the costume from a creative, practical and fit point of view. The supervisor may also consider it essential to invite a member of the wig team to first fittings, as the wigs need to be seen alongside the costume to check for proportion and the way the wig works with coat, shirt or blouse collars. Hats or headdresses may also need to be seen, for the same reason, so in a larger theatre, the costume prop team or milliners may need to be invited to the fitting at specific, pre-arranged points.

Occasionally, a toile can be used in rehearsal to test how well the design of the costume will work. In this situation, the supervisor will attend the rehearsal to receive feedback from the

Figure 8.4 A first toile fitting for *The Man of Mode*

Photograph: Margaret Maguire.

actor, director and designer. However, if the costume supervisor has not been able to attend any rehearsals prior to a workroom fitting, then it is a good idea to ask the actor whether they feel comfortable performing the stretches, dances or vigorous actions they have been performing in rehearsal. It is always important to observe the body language of the actors and gently question them about any problems or anxieties they may have about their costume. Look out for crossed arms, awkward silences or actors who pull at their costumes to express physical discomfort with what they are wearing. By calmly talking through their concerns, you should be able to make suitable adjustments and reach a resolution that is acceptable to everyone. Once fitted to the actor's body, the toile will now be used by the stitchers as a pattern to transfer to costume for the next stage of production, into 'top fabric', ready for the second fitting if you are lucky enough to have one scheduled.

SECOND FITTINGS

A second fitting may not be possible in every timeframe because of tight schedules for runs of the play in the latter stages of rehearsal. If you are fortunate enough to have the opportunity to arrange two separate fitting days, then your focus during the latter will generally be on finalizing trims, hemlines and accessories. Second fittings may also include fitting hired items from external rental or hire companies. Some of the costumes for *The Deep Blue Sea* were hired from London hire house Cosprop, and the actors attended fittings there which had been pre-arranged with the stage management team and the designer, Tom Scutt. Fitting hired costume also had to be managed by Maria Nicholson for *The Man of Mode*. Strong lines of communication with the deputy stage manager will be required to ensure the actors' availability and arrange these fittings. Inevitably, everyone in the creative team will be vying for the time of actors and technical staff during the penultimate or final week of rehearsal (when second fittings are usually scheduled). The lighting designer may wish to attend these fittings too, to see the color and the weight of fabrics used for some of the costumes, as these elements will certainly inform the overall lighting design. If you are working on a musical or dance show, then you should expect the choreographer to attend all fittings, as they naturally have a strong sense of how the costume will work with their choreography, and a very keen interest in the way a costume is worn and fits, as well as the overall line that can be achieved when the actor or dancer performs.

COSTUME PARADES

Nowadays, a costume parade is a relatively arcane practice in contemporary theatre. It involves taking all the actors out of rehearsal and dressing them in full costume, wigs, hair and make-up to assess how all the costumes look together in their groupings. The relationship of the costume to the set may also be examined by the creative team if the set is completed and safe for the actors to work on. A costume parade can be a very useful process for the designer and supervisor, as costumes can be checked for final adjustments to hemlines and fit before the tight deadlines of tech week. Accessories can be finally agreed on as well, and shoes and underpinnings can be checked for fit and their relationship to the top layer of costume. Often, changes will need to be made if there are visible unsightly bra or corset lines. Petticoats in period costume may also need to be adjusted if the actor cannot move easily or if waistbands are too uncomfortable. A costume parade was staged for *The Man of Mode*. The event was presented in a mirrored rehearsal room, as the site-specific venue away from the university campus did not allow for advance testing the costumes on the set. For actors, looking at themselves in costume in a large rehearsal or fitting room mirror can really help them to fully inhabit the finished costume – it may even act as a catalyst to complete their creative transformation.

There are several reasons why costume parades are now almost obsolete: the time that is taken to complete them eats into valuable rehearsal time. They are quite costly too, in person-hours and materials. Wigs and make-up costs, as well as costs for hosiery and extra cleaning, may be considerations for production managers and producers. Most significant, though, is the way contemporary theatre has evolved: actors are not seen as static individuals to be placed on the stage and looked at (even objectified) without the narrative and context of the play and the actors' parts to complete the storytelling. However, if the production manager and director are expecting a parade, then it is important to remember that the main role of the supervisor is to be organized, quick-thinking and communicate closely with the designer. The parade may save time, as the supervisor can get as many of the final costume notes completed satisfactorily before day one of tech week. If a parade results in numerous notes, then the supervisor will need to delegate to the team as required, by making copious lists of alterations, breaking down or dye room work, and shopping lists to give to buyers if more items need to be sourced and purchased. There are usually only two to three days in the schedule after a parade or final fittings to get everything done before the intensive work of tech week begins.

PRE-TECH REHEARSAL AND MEETING

In the run-up to tech week, in the final days of rehearsal, it is usual for complete runs of each act, and finally the whole play, to be performed to the creative and backstage teams, including the majority of the costume and running wardrobe staff. Watching this important final run rehearsal will obviously be helpful, and problems can be resolved before the tech week begins. The dressers also meet with the supervisor during the last week of rehearsal, to begin preparation for the tech and to allocate which dresser will be responsible for which actor, quick change and scene.

Stage management will give the supervisor and running wardrobe team an updated costume plot and scene-by-scene breakdown after the final rehearsal run. This plot will then be used by the dressers to finalize their quick change and dressing plots. On *The Deep Blue Sea*, there were three dressers, and each dresser looked after three to four actors. Student faculty productions like *The Man of Mode* may have many more dressers, with pantomime having fewer as a general rule. At a large theatre, the supervisor would now usually meet with the head of running wardrobe to establish final costume description lists of each element for each costume and to go through each costume rail together in preparation for the crucial pre-tech and tech stages of the production. As Michael Roff explained to me, in relation to *The Deep Blue Sea*:

> *It is very important that the costume supervisor communicates well with the running wardrobe team by using all possible means at their fingertips: written lists, verbal communication and photographs. The thing that really trips us up in the running wardrobe is when a costume supervisor just leaves us a rail of costumes with no detailed documentation.*[3]

The costume description list (Figure 8.5) will be used by the running wardrobe team to keep track of the costumes when they arrive backstage, and is a complete inventory of every item. If the supervisor provides a detailed list, it will help running wardrobe to manage the costumes for the run of the show. Additional information will also be added to the Costume Bible when the location and choreography of any quick changes (dressing room/stage/backstage) and precise method are established during the tech.

	A	B	C	D
1				
2	**Helen McCrory**	**Hester Collyer**	**throughout**	show bra
3				show pants
4				girdle
5				jonathan aston stockings
6				body stocking/ dance underwear (TBC)
7				waspie (TBC)
8				silver bracelet
9				gold watch
10				wedding ring
11			**A1**	slip
12				ballet pumps
13			*dresses on stage	silk flower print dressing gown OR burgendy dressing gown
14			**A2**	pale green silk blouse
15			QC 1min 30 (substage)	chartreuse silk pleated skirt
16			*soaked in rain	plum court shoes
17				blue flared coat
18				plum striped silk scarf
19				navy hat
20				russet corded handbag
21			* dresses on stage	skirt (as before)
22				russet lace knit jumper (removes blouse)
23				brown leather pumps
24			**interval**	
25			**A3**	slip (as before)
26			* dresses on stage	dressing gown (as before)
27				ballet pumps (as before)

Figure 8.5 Screenshot of a costume description list for *The Deep Blue Sea*

Source: Courtesy of the National Theatre, and created by Lucy Martin in Microsoft Excel.

NOTES

1 Michael Roff, interview and email correspondence with the author, 19 July 2016.
2 Pamela Howard, *What is Scenography?* (2nd ed., New York: Routledge, 2009), 166.
3 Michael Roff, interview and email correspondence with the author, 19 July 2016.

CHAPTER 9

Tech Week

Figure 9.1 Backstage rail and noticeboard

Photograph: Bill Bradshaw.

The technical rehearsal, or 'tech', is the first time the costumes will be seen and tested in practical and creative terms, with the set, props, lighting and sound all together in the correct order and context onstage. For costume supervisors, it is the time when they begin to hand over responsibility for looking after the costumes to the running wardrobe supervisor and the team of dressers, who will be maintaining the costumes for the performances. It can be a relief to finally get to this stage, but the handover to running wardrobe can also be a time of mixed emotions: letting go of the costumes that have been the focus of your attention for the last few weeks and seeing your work onstage at the same time. The running wardrobe team take the costumes to the next stage, and all have specific job roles that are outlined in Table 9.1, including head of running wardrobe, wardrobe supervisor, wardrobe assistant and dresser.

At first, the tech may be a little fraught, as the actors, the creative team and theatre management are all unsure how the production will develop in this critical week, or weeks. It is rare to be *absolutely sure* that your production will be a great success and that the collaborative work of all the participants will come together exactly as planned. There will inevitably be a perceptible feeling of concern about how the production will be received by the critics and audiences. The serendipity of theatre and the jeopardy inherent in this part of the process are among the factors that make tech week so exciting and everyone hyper-alert. Time is limited, and everyone has to be very focused and professional if they are to get through each entrance and cue on time. Perhaps because there are potentially so many unknown problems that may occur, the tech week has evolved to be very consistent in terms of schedule. In a mid-scale theatre or student faculty production, there will usually be a one-week tech period, as illustrated in Table 9.2. For a commercial production, or for a musical, the process may extend to two or even more weeks, with numerous previews. This is partly because the technical aspects of this scale of production will be necessarily much more complex and the financial and artistic stakes so high. Many changes will have to be made and technical cues thoroughly tested before the first night.

The days are very long at the tech – often with 12-hour calls – so the supervisor has a key role in keeping everyone one productive and on track. As Lucy Martin explained: 'Once you are in the tech, you need to step into the next stage of energy.'[1] Occasionally, the tech rehearsal will be the first time there has been a full run of the production. This is not an ideal situation, but is not uncommon. In these circumstances, keeping focused and calm is especially important for the supervisor, as actors, the director and designer can be concerned that there will not be enough time to get through everything before the scheduled dress rehearsal. A worried actor can easily become a very unhappy actor, and an actor's costume can quickly become an obvious area for criticism. The K for Kindness in ROCK is key at this stage.

During the tech front of house, the costume supervisor will be sitting with the designer and director. It is vital for supervisors to establish how lines of communication will work between themselves and the running wardrobe team before the tech begins. Most theatres should provide 'cans' or walkie-talkie communication to facilitate this. The costume supervisor needs to discuss with the running wardrobe supervisor how the daily notes will be managed and

Table 9.1 Running wardrobe job roles

Role	Job description	Duties
Dresser	Looks after the actors designated to them, making sure that they are dressed appropriately in accordance with the lists prepared by the costume supervisor and refined during the tech	Collects the costumes from the wardrobe and lays them out for actors in their dressing room, assisting them to dress if the costume is complex, then prepares all costume quick changes backstage and makes final checks in collaboration with the stage management team
		Assists with all quick changes, some of which may be onstage
		Maintains a tidy and organized backstage area
Head of running wardrobe	Liaises with the costume supervisor, running wardrobe team and the stage management team to make sure all the costumes are handled properly and efficiently so that the show can run as directed and designed	Manages the handover of the finished costumes and the successful running of the shows thereafter
		In a large theatre where there are numerous productions in repertory, manages a team of running wardrobe staff and dressers
		Arranges with their team to sort and archive costumes for future performances if there are plans for future staging, or the costumes will be returned to the costume stock/store at the end of a run
Wardrobe assistant	Prepares costumes for the performances	Collects costumes after performances, organizes repairs and laundering if required, and sorts them by character and scene in readiness for handover to the dressers
Wardrobe supervisor	Responsible for a specific show, making sure that costumes are correctly maintained and that the team are dressing actors correctly	Organizes teams of dressers and wardrobe assistants, replacing or repairing damaged or lost costumes in accordance with the requirements stipulated by the designer and laid down in the Costume Bible created by the original costume supervisor

Table 9.2 Typical tech week schedule

Day	Stage activity	Costume activity
1. Sunday	Rig lights, sound and get in and fit up the set	Costume are not usually on call
2. Monday	Continue fit up of the set Lights focused and the 'plotting' of each lighting state begins Sound is also plotted and checked The tech may begin in the evening	Costumes handed over to the running wardrobe team and prepared for distribution to the correct dressing rooms Dressers prepare for quick changes and begin to learn their individual dressing plot Actors dress in their costume and wigs
3. Tuesday	The tech begins or continues (a long day)	Actors dress in their costume and wigs
4. Wednesday	The tech continues, or if it has been completed by Day 3, then the morning can be allocated to technical work (set, lighting or sound) onstage **DRESS REHEARSAL 1 (afternoon or evening)** Production photography	Costume notes completed in the morning, and costumes cleaned, prepared and re-set for the dress rehearsal Wigs re-dressed and re-set Dressers on standby
5. Thursday	The morning can be allocated to technical work (set, lighting or sound) on stage. **DRESS REHEARSAL 2 (afternoon)** Notes from the director to actors and creative/backstage team Production photography **PERFORMANCE (or PREVIEW) 1** Notes with the director afterwards	Costume notes completed in the morning and costumes cleaned and prepared and re-set for the dress rehearsal Wigs re-dressed and re-set Dressers on standby
6. Friday	The morning can be allocated to technical work (set, lighting, sound) onstage **PERFORMANCE (or PREVIEW) 2** Notes with the director afterwards	Costume notes completed in the morning and costumes cleaned, prepared and re-set for the dress rehearsal Wigs re-dressed and re-set Dressers on standby Costume supervisor to hand over the Costume Bible to running wardrobe

completed during tech week. Will alterations be sent to the original stitchers in the workroom or handled by the running wardrobe team? It is important that these negotiations are handled carefully and diplomatically, and to remember that a supervisor must never take costumes from the rail or backstage without clearing this with the dressers. There can be a terrible panic if costumes seem to have disappeared from backstage!

So what actually happens in the tech? The purpose of the tech is to allow:

- the technicians to rehearse their part in the production and establish cues;
- the actors to practice working on the set in their costume, practicing their entrances and exits and using the props allocated to them;
- the designer to consider and refine their design and to work with stage management to rehearse scene changes;
- the dressers and actors to practice their quick changes;
- for refining the lighting levels and plotting the timing of cues;
- for the setting of sound levels, checking for audibility and the connection between lighting and sound;
- the deputy stage manager to record all the cues for the production in 'the book' before the dress rehearsal.

At the tech, the whole costume team, front of house and backstage, are watching to finalize every detail of costume and check that the actors are comfortable and dressed appropriately for each scene. The supervisor and running wardrobe team need to be very patient, as certain sections of action may be repeated time and time again until they are declared 'right' by the director and actor and 'safe' by stage management. The director will stop the action and say, 'Let's pause,' to go over any acting or technical concerns or details. The beginning of the tech is usually very, very slow, as everyone is trying to get used to the set, lighting, sound, special effects, costumes and props. The action will usually become smoother as the scenes progress and cues are learnt and repeated. The director will also learn how to find the desired effects and which technicians do what and when, so things tend to speed up considerably.

There can be a certain amount of experimentation at the tech, and the costume team will be looking carefully at all the costume items to see how they react under the lighting states: this is particularly true if, as on *The Deep Blue Sea*, there is a restricted color palette. There were three potential dressing gowns for Hester (Helen McCrory) to work with at the tech, and the supervisor and dressers had a key role in helping her to experiment with this costume element to see which felt right and communicated the correct physical appearance and psychological meaning. The supervisor and dressers have a key role in supporting actors and the designer in this important part of the creative process. As Michael Roff points out: 'Costume is not just about how it looks, it is also about how it makes the actor feel, which then feeds into their performance.'[2]

WORKING WITH THE RUNNING WARDROBE TEAM

During the tech, the supervisor will discuss and pass any dressing notes about changes to the running wardrobe supervisor. Keeping detailed notes is essential, as Lucy Martin confirms: 'Label everything very carefully and write everything down in a note pad throughout the rehearsal and tech week process. The make sure you accurately put this information into the Costume Bible as you go along.'[3]

The running wardrobe staff maintain the costumes and dress the actors on a daily basis during the run of a production. In the same way that the supervisor is responsible for turning the designer's vision into reality, the head of running wardrobe is responsible for keeping it that way during the run. The supervisor will have spent time with the running wardrobe, explaining how the costumes have been designed to look and work, any specialist maintenance requirements, and how to solve any problems that might emerge after first night. The costume supervisor and running team must work closely together during the tech to ensure a smooth and efficient handover. The supervisor might find it useful to create a 'notes template' that can be handed over to the running wardrobe team (for smaller alterations) and workroom (for more significant alterations). Headings for the template should include which actor and which costume, what needs fixing, the priority, and which department (costume shop, dye room, costume props or dressing team) should handle it.

The role of dressers is fundamental to any production (Figure 9.2). They work in close proximity to the actors, keeping them in good spirits and supported before the show begins and as they go onstage. Dressers are also responsible for choreographing the quick changes, some of which may be performed in hidden areas onstage, necessitating a long wait in or beside pieces of set for the deft change to happen, as if by magic. They must be very thorough about their work, and calm and cool-headed in an emergency or under pressure. Dressers must be good with people, be polite, but remain assertive at the same time. It is important that they maintain a good relationship with the stage management team too: this is vital, as both teams are working so closely together backstage. Dressing can be a rewarding job for all these reasons, and for many, it is the first stage in building a career in costume, and many costume supervisors start this way. As Michael Roff emphasizes:

> *Dressers have a great part in the production, and they love being in the darkness at the side of the stage, working to support the actors. . . . It might be useful to see the work of the running wardrobe department and dressing as the front line of costume. Never underestimate it, as the work of the dresser informs every aspect of costume in performance.*[4]

When working with actors as a dresser, it is important to maintain a light and efficient demeanor, maintain eye contact, and be respectful of the job the actor has to do. It takes a lot of preparation, nerve and skill to perform onstage. When working in the dressing room itself

Figure 9.2 Dressers backstage on *The Man of Mode*

Photograph: Bill Bradshaw.

(Figure 9.3), be aware that actors may be preparing for their roles, so keep an appropriate distance if you sense they want that, and a calm atmosphere if that seems to be what they need. As Lucy Martin advised: 'Try to maintain an easy and comfortable, yet professional, atmosphere onstage and backstage at all times.'[5]

The dressing team orchestrate quick changes, but will discuss them in the pre-tech meeting with the costume supervisor. Quick changes are sometimes difficult, but also an interesting challenge. Here are some useful tips for facilitating speedy quick changes:

Figure 9.3 A dressing room at the National Theatre

Source: Photograph courtesy of the National Theatre.

- Use elastic for shoe laces, or discuss choosing to use slip-on shoes with the designer and supervisor to speed up changes.
- Under-dress specific costume items if possible.
- Lay out the costumes to be changed very carefully, with the buttons and zips undone.
- Very quick-change adjustments to costumes will need to be planned for and made in the construction stages: buttons will be sewn on over front openings to disguise Velcro or popper/snap fastenings beneath. This type of technique is called a 'quick rig'.
- In pantomime, the traditional 'walk down' dame costumes (that usually require a very quick change) will often have heavy-duty zips sewn into the center-back seam, as part of a quick rig. The zips are rarely visible, as the 'walk down' costume is always performed 'out front' to the audience.
- A designer can design a quick change into some typical 'rags-to-princess gown' transformation, as seen in productions of *Cinderella*. The traditional rags costume can be gathered up to form a raggy polonaise that is then dropped by the actress as she performs a spin onstage to reveal a beautiful skirt below the rags. This, combined with a momentary pause offstage for the bodice to be pulled off by a dresser (perhaps all of this masked by lighting or smoke), reveals an underdressed sparkling bodice as if by magic.

Once the quick changes have been set in the tech and fully choreographed, a dressing plot is created, either by the dresser or supervisor. This document details the position of the changes and the setting of each item of costume for each change.

The dress rehearsal stage can be the first time when all the elements of the production are seen together. This can be a very exciting time for designers, as they can see the fruits of their labors at last. The atmosphere can feel as if it is palpably changing now that all the stage effects, lighting and sound work and performances are in sync. For the supervisor, it is important to look out for any problems with quick changes. Are the actors wearing what they should be, and does everything fit correctly? It almost certainly won't all be perfect, and there may still be one or two items that will have to be discreetly changed. It is very important not to impose too many changes on the actors at this late stage, as they have enough to contend with and remember without new costume items to worry about. Be sensitive to their needs and concerns – let the experienced dressers do their job to settle the actors.

The general rule for costume supervisors is that they provide costume consumables up to the first day of the run – socks, tights, insoles, haircuts – and after that, the running wardrobe have to provide the rest. The head of running wardrobe will have a budget for this, allocated by the head of costume or the production manager. However, recently introduced tax and revenue legislation in the UK allows for Value Added Tax to be reclaimed on consumables that are purchased *before* the first performance, which means that the National Theatre costume supervisors will be allocated budget that might have formerly been given to the running wardrobe to buy any anticipated goods to support the production during the run.

FITTING UNDERSTUDIES

Many supervisors try, and succeed, in fitting understudies before the first preview. However, it is not uncommon for understudies to be fitted after the dress rehearsal or first preview. Some costumes will be shared with the principal actors, but costumes for principals will usually be re-created as 'doubles' for understudies. Hester's chartreuse skirt in *The Deep Blue Sea* was re-created for her understudy as a bespoke item in the National Theatre workroom. However, it is acceptable (within UK Equity union rules) for the principal actors to share costume items with understudies as long as they are washable and not worn next to the skin. Shoes and any items in direct contact with the actor's body must be sourced for the exclusive use of an understudy. In an ideal world, the costume supervisor will have all the understudy costumes ready by the official first (press) night. Often, the casting of understudies will not be decided until well into the rehearsal period, and those designated may be of very different physical shape or size, so completely different costumes may have to be sourced. This is where the R for Resourceful in ROCK comes into play – particularly if the budget is restricted at this late stage in production. The theatre stores will be the first port of call. For student faculty productions, the runs are usually so short that there is generally little need for an understudy cast. Pantomime usually works a little differently, as the principal actors wear very elaborate and specific costumes that would have to be re-used if the dame was unwell. The careful use of T-shirts under the large costumes would be needed in this situation.

Opening night should be an exciting time for the whole costume team. For most supervisors, it is the end of the job, although in commercial theatre, the costume supervisor is kept on a retainer to manage the production after opening night (working with the full co-operation of running wardrobe). The preview is also the time for the handover of the final iteration of the Costume Bible, following reconciliation of the budget with the head of costume or production manager. Supervisor have to obtain final sign-off on all the financials and make absolutely sure that their designer is happy with all the costumes. Once all this is completed, the final installment of the fee should be paid.

The show will now be looked after by the running wardrobe team, who will make sure all the costumes are laundered, repaired (or replaced if irrecoverably damaged) and re-set each night, just as the supervisor has stipulated in the Costume Bible. When the final performance has been staged, the running wardrobe team will then use the Costume Bible inventory to cross-check which items are either drawn from or to be added to the theatre stock, or returned to external hire companies. They will also make a decision, in collaboration with the head of costume, about which items are to be disposed of. The 'return', as it is called, should be organized with precision, with hangers facing forward, sorted into groups (e.g. all shirts together). Costumes must be cleaned and checked thoroughly and repairs undertaken before they are sent on.

There remains nothing left to do now but to shut the Costume Bible up, hand it over, and get on with finding or starting that next job! The ephemeral nature of the costume supervisor's role must be borne clearly in mind at this stage, as the cycle begins again with a new production. The sheer exhilaration of theatre and the impermanence and jeopardy of this job can be both frustrating and joyful. Michael Roff sums it up perfectly when he says:

> *Theatre is a living thing, a living art form. It exists for the moment. What we are doing in theatre is enacting a leap of faith, and it relies on the collaboration of all the people onstage and backstage to work together to make the production and the art happen.*[6]

NOTES

1 Lucy Martin, interview and email correspondence with the author, 22 April 2016.
2 Michael Roff, interview and email correspondence with the author, 19 July 2016.
3 Lucy Martin, interview and email correspondence with the author, 22 April 2016.
4 Michael Roff, interview and email correspondence with the author, 19 July 2016.
5 Lucy Martin, interview and email correspondence with the author, 22 April 2016.
6 Michael Roff, interview and email correspondence with the author, 19 July 2016.

Epilogue

So much of the work of the costume supervisor relies on the individual being an organized, creative and generous person, so my approach has always been to try to develop these qualities in my own work and in my teaching. I hope this book goes some way to opening up the world of the costume shop and workroom for further scrutiny, with acknowledgement of the fundamental role that Costume (with a capital 'C') has in the theatre. As Pamela Howard carefully and accurately states, quoting the work of Korean scenographer Lee Byong-Boe: 'Theatre is nothing other than the dramatic images and stories that fill the vacuity of an empty space with the presence of the costumed actor.'[1]

Howard is acutely aware that performers feel extremely vulnerable when they are looking at their near-naked selves in a harshly lit mirror. Working as the creative collaborator with artists (actors, designers and directors) requires careful negotiation. Rehearsals, fittings and collaborative meetings all have the potential for unfortunate misunderstandings if handled insensitively by any of the participants. This book should go some way to presenting the methods costume supervisors use on a daily basis to help all the people they work with to feel completely supported and understood.

The intention of this book has also been to attempt to distil and evaluate what the supervisor does into a coherent whole, but writing it has been challenging because so little is published that accurately describes it. I hope this will begin that dialogue, but above all, that it has been a useful read for those who are starting out, and that those who already work in the field will be encouraged to see that a formal record has begun to be made about what a supervisor actually does.

Costume people are so generous, and I have found that there is a huge depth of knowledge to access and begin to describe and evaluate. This book just scratches the surface, and I wish I could have covered even more. What I have learnt is that costume supervisors are vital to the process of making theatre. They have to be flexible enough to respond to the creativity of everyone they work with, but focused enough to get the work onstage on time and on budget. It is a tricky and highly skilled juggling act to create a set of costumes that 'can compensate for [an actor's] real or imagined deficiencies'.[2] With all that to manage on a daily basis, it would do us all in the costume shop no harm once in a while to slap ourselves on the back and say, 'Well done!'

Figure E.1 Vintage cotton reels

Photograph: Margaret Maguire.

NOTES

1 Pamela, Howard, *What is Scenography?* (2nd ed., New York: Routledge, 2009), 168.

2 Ibid., 166.

Appendices

We are at the end of the book, but quite often I have referred to extra information as being listed in an appendix. These appendices contain examples of forms and templates, suppliers, fabric identification descriptions, sizing charts and a basic guide to starting an Excel spreadsheet that should be helpful for you to use in your journey as a costume supervisor.

Appendix 1: Fabric Identification Guide

Figure A.1.1 Broadwick Silks in Berwick Street, London

The descriptions below suggest the properties and textures of the most common fabrics you may encounter on your fabric sourcing expeditions, or in conversation with your costume designer, stitchers or actors.

Acetate: a man-made fiber derived from wood or cotton byproducts and then treated with acetic acid. It produces a durable, light-weight fabric that has a sheen, so it is often used in the production of **satins** and **taffetas**.

Acrylic: a man-made fiber that consists of a long chain of synthetic polymer.

Barathea: a worsted fabric that is traditionally used for fine tailoring. It has a natural ability to recover its shape, and is therefore very durable

Boucle: a fabric made with raised loops of yarn. It was used by Coco Chanel as a signature fabric in the creation of her iconic women's suits.

Brocade: a heavy, luxurious fabric with supplementary **jacquard** warp yarns or filling yarns, forming a slightly raised pattern often in a floral or scroll design. It is commonly used for costumes set before 1900.

Brocatelle: a heavy, luxurious fabric, similar to a **brocade**, but in a puffed-up or blistered pattern. Brocatelle has a heavy width-wise rib, and is usually used as a decorating fabric for draperies and upholstery.

Broderie anglaise: a cotton cloth that is embroidered with white thread to form a design of holes with the centers removed (often in white).

Buckram: a light-weight, plain-weave, open-construction, stiff, cotton-like fabric, used for costume and hat stiffening, **interfacing** and **interlining**.

Calico: a natural cream, light-weight, plain-weave cotton fabric used to make toiles (test garments). It can be bleached white.

Cambric: a light-weight, closely woven, plain-weave, linen-type fabric with a slight luster. It is used for linings.

Canvas: a heavy, plain, closely woven, durable, cotton-type fabric, used for industrial purposes (sails and tents) or as an **interlining** in tailoring.

Cashmere: a very costly, luxury wool woven from the downy hair from the undercoat of the cashmere goat of Tibet. It requires specialist dry cleaning.

Cavalry twill (UK): a medium-weight, durable, worsted-type fabric with prominent, fancy twill lines. It is traditionally used for period trousers and coats, especially military cavalrymen, hence its name.

Challis: a light-weight, plain-weave, slightly brushed, supple, woolen or cotton-type fabric, usually with a printed design, used for dresses, scarves and children's wear.

Chambray: a light-weight, plain-weave, cotton-type fabric usually with colored warp and white filling yarns, often in blue. It can have a square construction, and is commonly used for shirts.

Cheesecloth: a very light-weight, plain-weave, soft, cotton-type fabric that was very popular for clothes in the 1970's. It has a very open-weave construction.

Chenille: a textured but soft yarn made from a combination of wool, cotton or man-made fibers, commonly used for women's scarves.

Chiffon: a light-weight, sheer, plain-weave, silk-like fabric with filament yarns that are highly twisted, usually used for dresses and blouses.

Chino: a medium-weight, closely woven, twill-weave, cotton-type fabric, often used for uniforms and trousers.

Chintz: a light/medium-weight, plain-weave, closely woven, fine cotton fabric, imported from India, with a glazed (polished) finish, usually printed in bright colors with a pale white or cream background. It is often used in soft furnishings rather than clothing, although it was popular in the Victorian period for dresses.

Corduroy: a medium-weight cotton fabric with a length-wise raised surface produced by cutting the pile filling yarns. It is often used for country-style or casual jackets and trousers.

Crepe: a fabric with a crinkled surface, made using high-twist yarns, chemicals or weave. Variations include **crepe de chine** and **georgette**.

Crepe de chine: a **satin** fabric with a **crepe** surface on the dull (back) side.

Crinoline (crin): a light-weight, plain-weave, stiff, cotton-type or synthetic fabric with a very open construction, used for supporting hoop skirts or hem edges and **interlining**.

Crushed velvet: a **velvet** fabric in which the surface has been flattened to give a crushed effect that reflects light with light and dark areas.

Damask: a firm, lustrous fabric with a reverse **jacquard** design on both sides. It is flatter than **brocade**, and is suitable for historical costume.

Denim: a medium-weight, twill-weave, cotton-type fabric, with a colored warp and white or gray filling. The traditional color is indigo blue, which usually begins to fade after a few washes. It is used for jeans and work clothes.

Doeskin: a lustrous, easily draping fabric that has the appearance and feel of the skin of the female deer. Rain can run off doeskin in the direction of the nap, which lends it to coat and jacket design.

Dotted Swiss: a light-weight cotton (usually white) with dots or tufts, often used for late Victorian summer dresses.

Double knit: a knitted fabric of double thickness with the same finish on both sides.

Drill: a durable cotton fabric with a twill weave, similar to **denim**, used for work clothes.

Duchess satin: a very costly, heavy, rich-looking **satin** fabric with a shiny, silky sheen, used for wedding dresses and ball gowns.

Duffle: a soft, heavy-weight wool/**Nylon** mix, named after the town in Belgium where the fabric originates. It is traditionally used for duffle coats, made famous by the British Navy. The coats have large horn or wooden toggles and corded fastenings.

Dupion: often silk, a rough uneven weave with heavy 'slub', dyed in bright colors and consequently very popular for costume use, but can be prone to damage and wear and tear.

Faille: a medium-weight, semi-lustrous cotton fabric with very noticeable cross-wise ribs, often used for evening dresses.

Faille taffeta: **taffeta** with very visible cross-wise ribs.

Felt: a dense matted wool with a 'pressed' appearance. It can be used for surface decoration and for hats, and occasionally for making costume.

Flannel: a light/medium-weight, soft cotton or woolen-type fabric, usually brushed on both sides.

Fleece: a woven fabric, often produced from man-made fibers, ideal for casual wear and dressing gowns. It does not fray.

Foulard: a silk fabric with a narrow width (often 73cm/28in), used for ties.

Gabardine: a medium-weight, fine-yarn, durable, twill-weave fabric with slight twill lines. Cotton or worsted types are traditionally used for trousers, suits and raincoats.

Gauze: a very light, sheer, open-construction, plain-weave, cotton-type fabric. It is often used for net curtains and bandages.

Georgette: a light, sheer fabric with a dull **crepe** surface – often silk. It is sometimes called crepe georgette).

Gingham: a light-weight, plain-weave, cotton-type fabric, usually with a plaid or check pattern, used for country-style dresses and shirts.

Grosgrain: a heavy, closely woven, lustrous fabric with pronounced cross-wise ribs, used for shoes, ties, ribbons, graduation gowns and vestments in churches.

Habotai (UK): a very light-weight, plain-weave silk fabric, often also referred to as 'parachute silk'.

Harris Tweed: the trademark for tweed fabrics made exclusively in the islands of the Outer Hebrides, off the north-west coast of Scotland. It is primarily used for men's sports jackets.

Hessian: **(US, burlap)**: a coarse material used for sacking or upholstery. It has some uses in costume to re-create distressed rags and aprons. It is also referred to as 'jute'.

Hound's tooth or dog's tooth: a broken check effect, often in an over-sized design, usually in monochrome. It can create a very dramatic appearance when used for tailoring.

Interfacing: fabrics used as reinforcement between inner lining and outer surface fabrics. Some have a surface treatment that 'glues' the two fabrics together when ironed (described as 'fusible').

Interlining: stiff **linen** canvas used in tailoring for jackets and coats. It is also used to describe a material used to add warmth and weight to clothing.

Jacquard: a fabric in which the warp thread is raised during weaving so that an intricate design is created in one color.

Jersey: a knitted, stretchy fabric sometimes woven in a tube, or flat warp knitted.

Khaki: a heavy-weight, yellow-brown-green cotton or wool fabric, traditionally used for British Army uniforms since the mid-19th century. It is now a ubiquitous color and fabric for fashion casual wear.

Lace: a fabric in which threads are interwoven to create intricate and delicate patterns or designs. It is used either as an overlay for dresses or as a trimming for blouses or shirts.

Lamé: a metallic, shiny fabric, often in gold or silver, often used in evening wear in the 1930's.

Lawn (UK): a light-weight, fine, plain-weave, cotton-type fabric that is slightly stiff. It is a little less sheer than **voile**, and is used for blouses and dresses, particularly for Victorian clothing.

Linen: a natural fiber made from the flax plant. It is absorbent and wicks moisture from the body, so it is traditionally used for clothing worn in the tropics. It crinkles after wearing, and can be used to create a 'period' look for theatre.

Lycra: a trademarked stretch, knitted fabric made from cotton or synthetic yarn, used for dancewear. In the United States, the term Spandex is more commonly used.

Marquisette: a light-weight, sheer, open-construction weave, similar to mosquito netting.

Melton: a heavy-weight, closely woven woolen fabric, completely felted with nap, used for coats and uniforms. Also: melange melton – a melton with a marbled effect, achieved by adding different-colored fibers to the raw blend of the wool, traditionally used for collars in coats, but also for the whole coat design.

Mohair: a fabric woven from the wool of the angora goat, with a soft, hairy quality. It is often woven with regular wool, and is used for millinery or suits.

Muslin: a light- to medium-weight, plain-weave, stiff, unfinished cotton fabric with a speckled effect. When finished, the fabric is soft and drapes easily.

Moiré: a finish for a range of fabrics, from silk and cotton to man-made fibers, that adds a swirling pattern, reflecting light. It is usually a stiff, crisp and rustling fabric, predominantly used for Victorian or contemporary evening dress.

Moleskin: a warm, thick fabric with a soft, napped surface. It has the appearance of suede in some instances, and is predominantly used for menswear and tailoring.

Net: a mesh fabric that can be either very stiff or soft, made from fibers ranging from silk to man-made. It is an essential material in the making of ballet tutus (sometimes called **tulle**) and period underpinnings, petticoats and evening dress.

Nylon: a strong, synthetic fabric, invented before WWII, but widely commercially available after 1945. It is a very durable material that has revolutionized the fashion industry. Sometimes the word is used to describe women's hosiery.

Ombre: a graduated and shaded color effect from dark to light.

Organdie: a light-weight, plain-weave, cotton-type, open-construction fabric with fine-spun yarns and a stiff finish.

Organza: similar to **organdie**, except made of silk or man-made fiber, often used for dresses and trimmings.

Ottoman: a silk or man-made luxury fabric with heavy corded ribs that run lengthways.

Oxford cotton: a light-weight, soft, cotton-type fabric with small basket-weave repeats and fine warp and coarse filling yarns, with a smooth surface. It is often used for the traditional 'Brooks Brothers'-style button-down collared shirts.

Panné: typically a **velvet** with a flattened long pile, creating a lustrous sheen, used in the early part of the 20th century for women's clothes and accessories.

Percale: a light-weight, plain-weave, fine-yarn, combed, cotton-type fabric, primarily used for sheets, dresses and blouses.

Pilot cloth: a wool cloth traditionally used for jackets worn by seamen. It is often abbreviated to 'P-cloth' or 'pea coat', made famous by beatniks in the 1950's and 1960's.

Plaid (US): see **Tartan**.

Polyester: a highly durable fabric created using man-made polymers.

Poplin: a crisp cotton fabric, predominantly used for shirts and dresses. It is ribbed with a mercerized yarn in the warp.

Sateen: a medium-weight, cotton-type fabric with a **satin** weave and lustrous surface, used for trousers and shoe uppers.

Satin: a medium-weight fabric, often silk. Satin weave has fine, closely woven warp yarns, a highly lustrous, shiny smooth face and a dull, rougher back. It is commonly used for 1930's evening dresses, and varieties include crepe-back satin, **duchess satin** and slipper satin.

Scrim: a very light-weight, sheer, open-construction, plain-weave, cotton-type fabric, similar to a slightly stiff **cheesecloth**.

Seersucker: made of cotton or synthetic fibers, this fabric has stripes of yarn which are crinkled. Best suited to blouses and dresses, it can also be used for men's summer jackets.

Serge: a heavy, worsted-type, durable, solid-colored, smooth-surfaced fabric with a twill weave, used for suits.

Shantung: a medium-weight, plain-weave silk fabric with a heavy textured surface that can suit costume that has an oriental style.

Taffeta: a medium-weight, plain-weave, shiny fabric with slight cross-wise ribs. It has great rustle, and is often used for evening dresses and women's suits.

Tapestry: a heavy-yarn, ribbed fabric with a colored **jacquard** design resulting from different-colored groupings of filling yarns (visible as stripes on the fabric back), made with two sets of warp yarns and two sets of filling yarns.

Tartan (UK): a woven wool originating in Scotland, with colorful checks, used for kilts and suits.

Ticking (UK): a heavy, strong, closely woven, cotton-type fabric, usually made with stripes or a woven design, traditionally used for mattresses and bed pillows.

Tulle: a very fine, slightly stiff, silky, net-like fabric, used for wedding veils, ballet costume and trimmings.

Tweed: a medium/heavy-weight, woolen, rough twill-weave fabric with a fuzzy surface and colored rough yarn, used for suits. Varieties include Donegal Tweed, Harris Tweed, Irish Tweed and Scottish Tweed.

Velour: a medium-weight, cotton-type, dense, cut-pile fabric that resembles **velvet**, often used in fashion sportswear.

Velvet: a medium-weight silk or synthetic fabric with a cut-pile surface.

Voile: a light-weight, semi-transparent, crisp, plain-weave, high-twist, spun-yarn, cotton-type fabric with very, very fine yarns, used for women's summer dresses and for sheer curtains.

Zibeline: a lustrous fabric that is often made from wool, **mohair** or camel hair. It is a luxury fabric with a stiff, but still soft, quality that makes it very useful for evening dresses and capes.

Appendix 2: The Costume Supervisor's Contract

This is an example of a typical costume supervisor's contract when working within an established theatre. Please note that the content and terms will naturally change from institution to institution and from country to country. The example here assumes standard payment in thirds, with the handover of the Costume Bible and the finalization and approval of the finances with the Head of Costume or Production Manager, generally accepted as the end of the contract. Note the detail concerning liaison with the 'costume administrator' in the final paragraphs of the supervisor's contract. This aspect describes specific financial processes applied by the theatre that provided this sample contract, relating to credit cards, sales taxes and final reconciliation. In the UK, sales tax was 20% at the time of writing, but naturally this figure will change in the future. Quantities of sales tax may vary quite dramatically from nation to nation. In the US, sales tax is governed and levied at state level so it will vary by region, with some states eliminating it all together. Value Added Tax (as it is called in the UK) is collected by the retailer and so costume supervisors will need to agree with their employer whether it is to be added to finalised budgets or not (see notes on budgeting in Chapter 5). Readers are advised to look back to Chapter 4 for details about 'Setting up cashflow and finance for your production', with advice about asking employers to state in the contract exactly what extra items are the supervisor's responsibility e.g. personal transport, packing and shipping of goods and public liability insurance.

Theatre logo

Name & address
Date

Dear [Name],

I would like to confirm your engagement as Costume Supervisor for the [Show title] Theatre Production of [name of show] directed by [director] and designed by [designer].

Rehearsals begin on [date]; the technical rehearsals on [date] and the previews will begin on [date]. The press night will take place in the [theatre] on [date]. You will be issued with [one/two] tickets for press night.

I would like to offer you a fee of [full fee amount] and payment will be made in **three instalments**. The first instalment of [1/3 fee] is due [date]; the second instalment of [1/3 fee] will be due in the week beginning [date]; and the third instalment of [1/3 fee] will be due on completion of the project, along with proof of credit card and petty cash float clearance and a completed Costume Bible. The invoices must be submitted by you to the Finance Department. You are personally responsible for your payment of tax and national insurance.

You will be expected to manage your hours in a way which is most effective for yourself and the production to ensure the successful completion of your contract (including understudies), finishing on the press night or the conclusion of the project, whichever is the later. Please inform me of any periods of unavailability during your contracted time. Your show buyer for this project is [buyer name].

You are responsible for the costume budget and you must have authorisation from the Head of Costume/Production Manager for any orders that will exceed [add figure]. Any problems which might result in the budget being exceeded must be brought to the attention of the Head of Costume/Production Manager before you commit the theatre to any order. You will be issued with a credit card and are responsible for keeping all receipts relating to purchases as well as registering any spending with our finance department.

You will be required to attend a weekly costume workshop meeting on [date] to update on progress. You will be required to update your show budget sheet for this meeting which is held on our in-house finance system – guidance will be given on this process.

Either on or before the first day of rehearsals you MUST make yourself available to the Costume Administrator, to have an induction; talk through health and safety regulations, and discuss the processes and procedures of the department. You will also be issued with a temporary staff card and departmental keys. You will also be required to attend an exit meeting to make sure all paperwork and financial transactions are in order before you leave.

If for any reason you are unable to fulfil this engagement, we reserve the right to make alternative arrangements.

A temporary staff card will be issued to you. This must be returned to the Costume Office as soon after press night as possible, together with any departmental keys issued to you. A deposit will be charged on issue of staff card and keys, returnable on their return. If you accept this offer you should sign the enclosed copy and return it to me.

Yours sincerely,

Head of Costume

Figure A.2.1 A typical costume supervisor's contract

Appendix 3: Male and Female Measurement Forms

Chapter 6 discussed the merits of using a gender-neutral measurement form. Here are the alternative traditional measurement forms that may be preferred by some supervisors.

Table A.3.1 Male measurement form

Production:		Date:	
Artist:		Character:	
Cutter:			

Height:		Wrist:	
Neck:		Around hand:	
Lower neck:		Outside leg to knee:	
Chest:		Outside leg to ground	
Waist:		Inside leg to knee:	
Seat:		Inside leg to ground:	
Across chest:		Rise (outside leg to ground minus inside leg to ground):	
Nape to waist (front):		Around thigh:	
Across back:		Around knee:	
Half across back to elbow		Below knee:	
Half across back to wrist		Around calf:	
Nape to waist (back):		Around ankle:	
Nape to jacket length:		Head circumference:	
Nape to knee:		Ear to ear:	
Nape to ground:		Hairline to nape:	
Shoulder:		Shoe size:	
Around armhole:		Gloves:	
Scye:		Notes:	
Arm length:			
Arm around top:			
Arm around forearm:			

Table A.3.2 Female measurement form

Production:		Date:	
Artist:		Character:	
Cutter:			

Height:		Arm length:	
Neck:		Arm around top:	
Lower neck:		Arm around forearm:	
Bust:		Wrist:	
Under bust		Outside leg to knee:	
Waist:		Outside leg to ground	
Hip:		Inside leg to knee:	
Across chest or back width:		Inside leg to ground:	
Point to point:		Rise (outside leg to ground minus inside leg to ground):	
Nape to bust point:		Around thigh:	
Nape to under bust:		Around knee:	
Nape to waist (front):		Below knee:	
Nape to waist (back:)		Around calf:	
Nape to jacket length:		Around ankle:	
Nape to ground:		Head circumference:	
Across back:		Ear to ear:	
Half across back to elbow		Hairline to nape:	
Half across back to wrist		Shoe size:	
Shoulder:		Gloves:	
Around armhole:		Notes:	
Scye:			

Appendix 4: Standard Size Charts

It is very important to use charts these only as a *guide* when sourcing clothing, as sizes will vary between different manufacturers. They are very useful if you find you have a 'rogue' measurement that does not make sense to you after you have finished measuring your actors. By comparing all the other measurements to these charts, you may be able to ascertain whether the measurement that does not make sense has been recorded incorrectly, or whether there is going to be a problem with making for that performer.

Table A.4.1 Male size guide form

United States and United Kingdom	Europe	Chest (inches)	Waist (inches)	Neck/shirt sizes (inches)	Sleeve lengths (inches)	Leg lengths
34 [XS]	44	33–34	27-28	13–13½	31½–32	Will be determined in inches:
36 [S]	46	35–37	29-31	14–14½	32½–33	Short = 29
38 [M]	48	38–40	32-34	15–15½	33½–34	Regular = 31–32
40 [L]	50	42–44	36-38	16–16½	34½–35	Long = 34
42 [XL]	52	46–48	40-42	17–17½	35½–36	Extra long = 36
44 [XXL]	54	50–52	44-46	18–18½	36–36½	
46 [XXXL]	56	54–56	50-52	19–19½	36½–37	

Table A.4.2 Female size guide form

Letter sizes	United States	United Kingdom	Europe	Bust (in/cm)	Waist (in/cm)	Hips (in/cm)	Leg lengths (in)
XS	2	6	32	30/76	22/58	33/84	Short = 28–29
S	4	8	34	32/81	24/61	35/89	Regular = 30–31
S	6	10	36	34/86	26/66	37/94	Long = 32–33
M	8	12	38	36/91	28/71	39/99	Extra long = 34–35
M	10	14	40	38/97	30/76	41/104	
L	12	16	42	40/102	32/81	43/109	
L	14	18	44	42/107	34/86	45/114	
XL	16	20	46				
1XX	18	22	48				
2X	20	24	50				
3X	22	26	52				
4X	24	28	54				

Table A.4.3 Shoe size guide

Women's			Men's		
United States	Europe	United Kingdom	United States	Europe	United Kingdom
4	35	2	6	39	5.5
4.5	35	2.5	6.5	39	6
5	35–36	3	7	40	6.5
5.5	36	3.5	7.5	40–41	7
6	36–37	4	8	41	7.5
6.5	37	4.5	8.5	41–42	8
7	37–38	5	9	42	8.5
7.5	38	5.5	9.5	42–43	9
8	38–39	6	10	43	9.5
8.5	39	6.5	10.5	43–44	10
9	39–40	7	11	44	10.5
9.5	40	7.5	11.5	44–45	11
10	40–41	8	12	45	11.5
10.5	41	8.8	13	46	12
11	41–42	9	14	47	13.5
11.5	42	9.5	15	48	14.5
12	42–43	10	16	49	15.5

Table A.4.4 Glove size guide

Men's			Women's		
Size	in	cm	Size	in	cm
XS	7	18	XS	6	15
S	7½–8	20	S	6½	16.5
M	8½–9	23	M	7	18
L	9½–10	25	M/L	7½	19
XL	10½–11	28	L	8	20
XLL	11½–12	30	XL	8½	23

Appendix 5: Creating a Document Using Excel

Excel is the program most frequently used to create spreadsheets. Costume Supervisors use Excel spreadsheets for: costume breakdowns, Costume Description Lists, Budgeting and Finance records. The images and instructions below have been based on originals created by my colleague Technician Demonstrator and Costume Supervisor, Helen Ford.

1. Start with a newly opened 'Book' with Book 1 showing: more Books can be added by using the '+' symbol (Figure A.5.1).

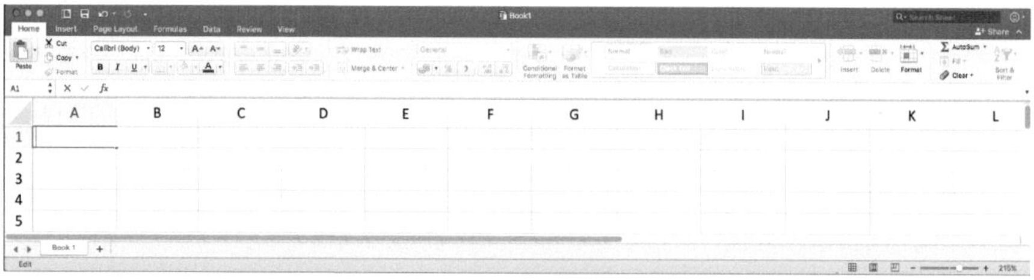

Figure A.5.1 A newly opened Excel 'Book'

2. Click with the mouse in the first 'cell', A1 and add an appropriate title for the sheet – e.g. 'Budget Breakdown' (Figure A.5.2).

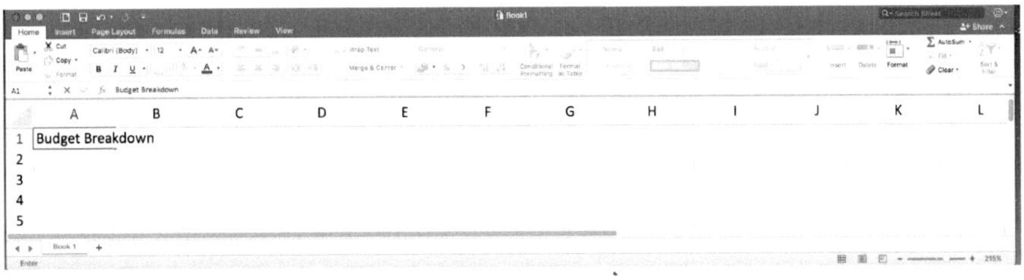

Figure A.5.2 Creating the first cell

3. Format the title by selecting the words and then 'B' for Bold (Figure A.5.3).

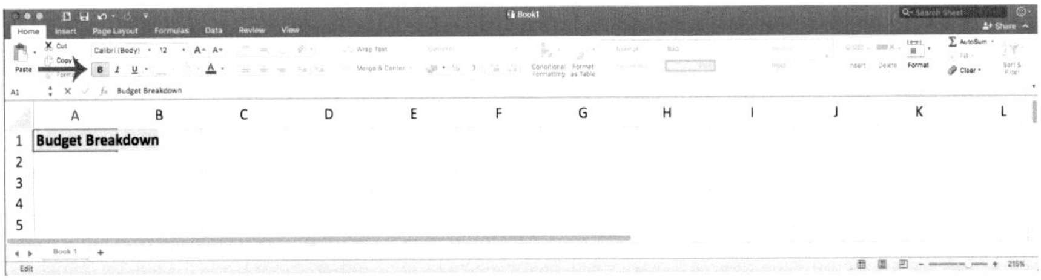

Figure A.5.3 Formatting the title

4. Center the title across the columns by selecting them followed 'Merge and Center' (Figure A.5.4).

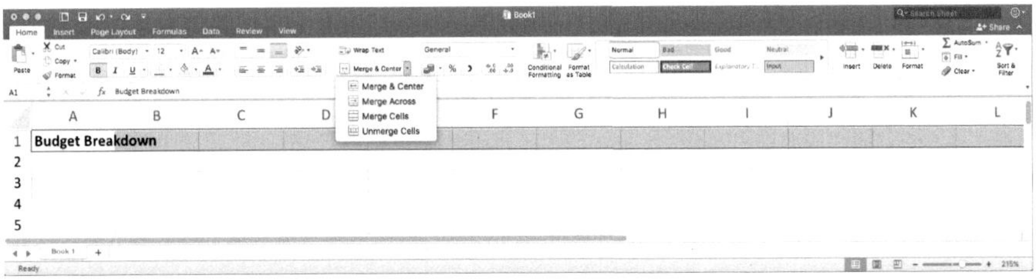

Figure A.5.4 'Merge and Center'

5. Add the headings you need e.g. Artist, Character, Act etc - then click with the mouse in cells A2 and B2 and type the text (Figure A.5.5).

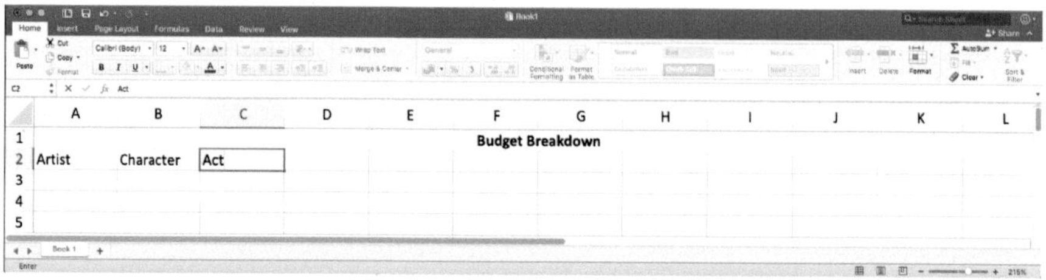

Figure A.5.5 Adding Headings

6. To adjust column widths, double-click on the right hand of the column edge or click on the line and drag across (Figure A.5.6).

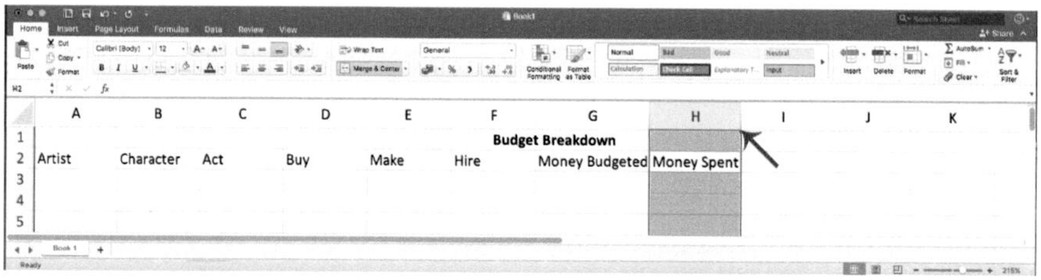

Figure A.5.6 Adjusting column widths

7. Continue adding your columns headings, adjusting widths in the process (Figure A.5.7).

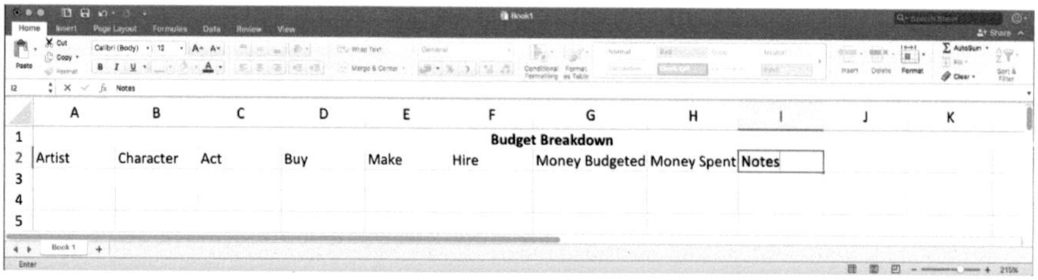

Figure A.5.7 Continue to add Headings

8. To name the worksheet, click on the sheet tab name and select the 'rename' menu option. For example, change it to 'Budget Breakdown' (Figure A.5.8).

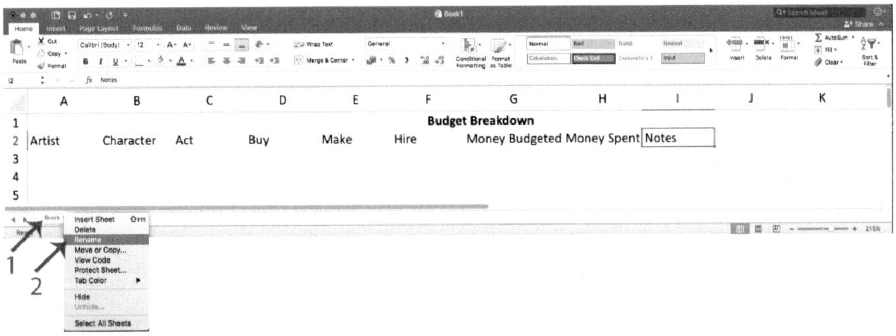

Figure A.5.8 Naming the Worksheet

9. For example, change it to 'Budget Breakdown + your production title' (Figure A.5.9).

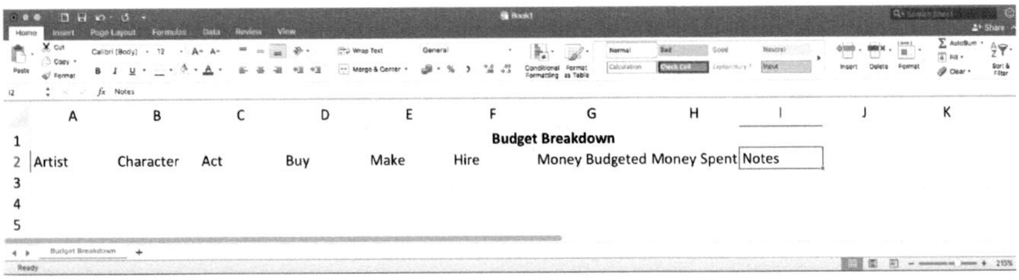

Figure A.5.9 Changing Titles

10. Save the work you have created so far, by clicking on the 'Diskette' icon, then 'File', then 'Save as' (Figure A.5.10).

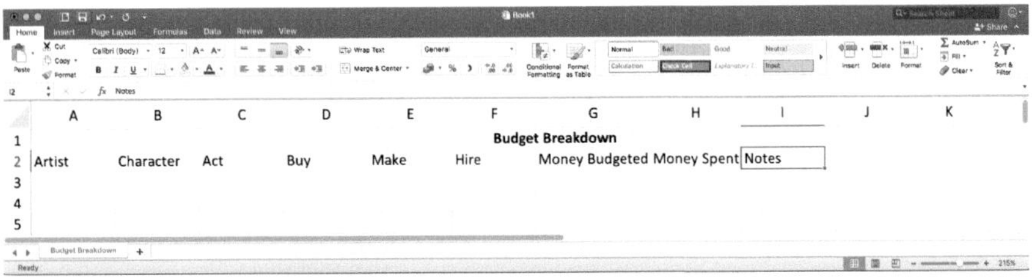

Figure A.5.10 Saving the Worksheet

11. Finally, choose a suitable filename and location (Figure A.5.11).

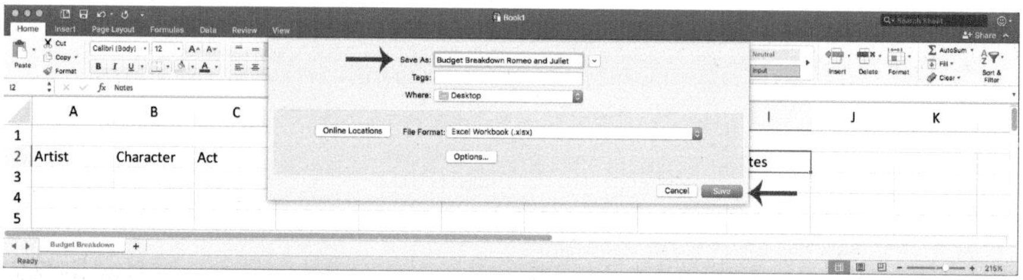

Figure A.5.11 Choosing the Filename

12. To enter data into the spreadsheet, you can simply fill each cell with the information that relates to your production. Then click on the 'General' icon and select 'Currency' (choose one e.g. $). Then move across each number and select the currency for that number (Figure A.5.12).

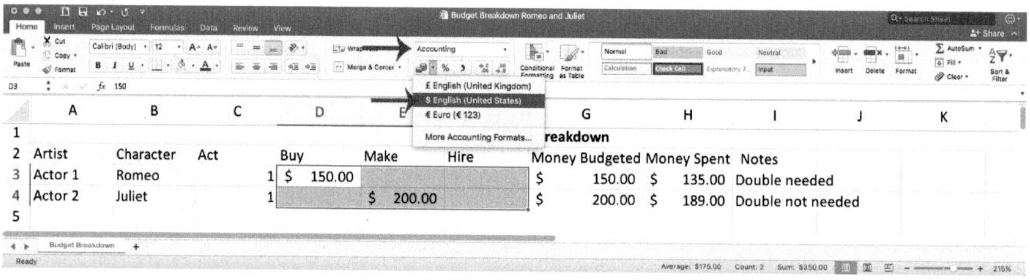

Figure A.5.12 Selecting a Currency

13. To use the power of Excel to calculate totals in the 'Money Budgeted' column, you can highlight the figures you want to calculate and then click the 'AutoSum' icon. You now have the basic skills required to begin using spreadsheets for all your costume supervision projects (Figure A.5.13).

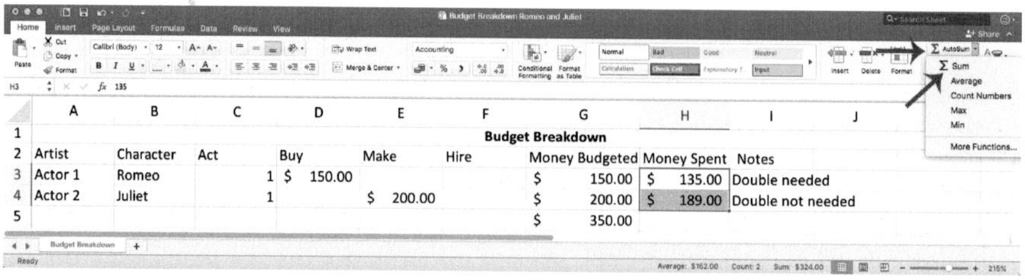

Figure A.5.13 Adding sums together using 'Auto Sum'

Glossary

Glossary 1 Fabrics in Berwick Street

Photograph: Margaret Maguire.

This list defines and describes some of the numerous terms that relate to theatre practice, the rehearsal period and tech week, as well as the costume and workroom.

ASM: assistant stage manager, the most junior member of the stage management team.

Auditorium: the Latin name for the space in the theatre where the audience are seated or spectate from during the performance.

Beginners: the announcement made by the **DSM** five minutes before curtain up to alert the actors appearing in the first scene to come to the stage because the performance will begin imminently.

Blacks: the term given to long black serge cloths hung to conceal the sides of the stage from view.

Blocking: term used to describe the precise arrangement of movements and actions performed by the actor, but arranged during rehearsal by the director and then noted by the **DSM** in the **book**.

Book: the annotated script that details every action, lighting and sound effect and set change, written up by the **DSM**.

Borders: the term given to the wide black cloths or hard scenery used to conceal the lights above the stage from view.

Breakdown artist: the costume team member who works to distress or age the costumes so that they do not look too new and have an aura of the character who inhabits them.

Buyer: the costume team member who shops for the production, under the direction of the costume supervisor.

Call: the warning given to actors and technicians that they are soon to be needed onstage and backstage. Also the email or daily call sheet that will announce who will be rehearsing that day and at what time.

Cans: the headsets provided for the technical crew that allow for communication during the performance.

Costume Bible: A file that is created by the costume supervisor by the end of the **preview** period that includes contact details, measurement forms, photographs of the actors, fitting information, quantities and fabric swatches, descriptions of all suppliers, fabrics and notions, hire details, sourcing information, finance and budget information.

Costume description list: a list created by the costume supervisor of each costume element for each actor. The list is handed over to the **running wardrobe** team for the **tech** rehearsal.

Costume design/plate/sketch: the drawing created by the designer to indicate how the costume will look. It will be annotated and labeled with the relevant act and scene.

Costume plot: a table with all aspects of the costume for each character in the play, described act by act and scene by scene. This is usually created by the stage management team prior to the tech, but a version should also be made by the costume supervisor before the first rehearsal.

Costume stock (UK, costume store): the collection of costumes that are held by the theatre or a rental/hire department.

Cue: the signal point at which an action or stage effect takes place. It can be a verbal or physical signal (**cue light**).

Cue light: a box with a red (stand by) and green (go) light that indicates to an actor or technician when to perform an action.

Cue sheet: a list of the particular effects performed by a department in a production.

Curtain call: the moment when all the actors take to the stage to receive applause at the end of the show.

Curtain up: announcement given to the technicians that the show has begun.

Cutter (US, draper): the costume team member who drafts the patterns from the costume designs. The cutter then oversees the manufacture of the costumes.

Cutting on the stand: method used to create a pattern on a mannequin/dress form using calico or a similar cheap fabric and pins.

Double: a situation when two costumes are required to be made to allow for a particular special effect or for two actors to perform the same role in one play.

Dress parade: the final look at the costumes by the creative team before the **tech** week begins. It is not practiced that often nowadays.

Dress rehearsal: the final run of the production without an audience, in full costume.

Dressers: members of the **running wardrobe** team who prepare the costumes and assist the performers to dress, both in their dressing rooms and for quick changes onstage and backstage.

DSM: deputy stage manager, the member of the stage management team who works closely with the director in the rehearsal room to annotate the blocking and staging so that they can then 'call' the show from the prompt corner during performances.

Dye room: the space in the costume shop where fabrics are dyed or distressed, using various processes.

Entrance: the place onstage where the actor enters.

Exit: the place where the actor leaves the stage.

First night: the performance after the **previews**, when the critics come to review the show, the costume supervisor's work is complete and the **Costume Bible** is handed over.

Fit up: the days before the **tech** week, when the set is built onstage.

Fitting: the process of trying the costume on the actor and adjusting it to fit as envisioned by the designer. There may be first and second fittings. The costume supervisor arranges the fittings with the stage management team.

Fitting room: the space where the costumes are tried on by the actor, with the designer and costume supervisor present. Creative and practical decisions are made in this space.

Flat (also flattage): the units of scenery that make up the set.

Flies: the space above the stage where bars are hung for scenery and lighting.

Fly floor: the gallery high above the stage from which the flies are operated.

Flying: the process of bringing in and out scenery or an actor by wires from the space above the stage.

Focusing: the process of establishing and adjusting each light to create an exact effect onstage.

Get in/out: the term given to the arrival of the set, costumes and lighting to the stage and removal afterwards.

Iron: the metal fireproof curtain that can be lowered to divide the auditorium from the stage in the event of a fire or emergency.

Measurement comparison sheet: a chart, formatted as a table, that lists the measurements for each performer in a convenient and easily accessible format.

Mic pack: the small bag used to conceal the receiver pack worn by actors if they are having their voices amplified by radio microphones (radio mics).

Mood board: the collection of visual imagery a costume designer may opt to use to communicate their ideas to the creative team.

Petty cash: an advance of cash to cover production goods and costs.

Plotting: the process of establishing each action or effect in the play, such as lighting, sound or costume changes.

Preview: the performances after the dress rehearsal, but before the first night. A preview has an audience, but the action may be interrupted and practical details can change.

Prop costume: costumes that have specific mechanical or practical dimensions. A large sports mascot might be described as a prop costume, as might a pantomime cow or dame costume.

Purchase order: a legally binding order between a supplier and a buyer. It details the items that have been ordered and the price point agreed.

Quick change: a costume change performed backstage by dressers to create a seamless flow of action from moment to moment within the play. It will usually be heavily choreographed and rehearsed, and a quick change area may need to be created in the **wings** to accommodate the quick change.

Quick rig: a costume that has been specifically altered to make adjustments to facilitate a very quick change.

Rehearsal notes: the list of requirements that have emerged from that day of rehearsal. The notes are divided into departments – general, set, lighting, sound, props and costume – and are written up by the **DSM**.

Running wardrobe: the team who manage the costumes once the show is onstage and in performance.

SM: stage manager, in control of the performances and manager of the stage management team.

Strike: the removal of set and/or costumes from the stage.

Swatch: the small cuttings of fabric positioned by the costume designer on their designs to indicate which fabrics are used where. Supervisors and buyers may also 'swatch' the show for the designer, so that decisions can then be made back at the **workroom** about which fabrics to order.

Tech: abbreviation of '(technical)', the period of days or a week when the production is rehearsed onstage and all aspects of the staging (set, costume, lighting and sound) are explored, learnt and tested.

Toile (US, muslin): the draper/cutter will create a first practice version of the design on a mannequin from calico or a cheap fabric. This is then discussed with the designer and used to create a new version from the desired fabric (top fabric).

Traverse: a type of staging in which the audience are seated in parallel seating blocks opposite each other, with the acting area between them.

Truck: a wheeled platform used to place a piece of set to facilitate movement onstage and offstage.

Wig oven: a hot cabinet used to set wigs after they have been dressed and prepared by the wig master/mistress.

Wig room: the wig department area, usually beside the costume **workroom**.

Wings: the spaces to the left and right of the stage where actors wait to go onstage and where **quick changes** may be performed. The wings are usually concealed from view by large flats or stage cloths called **blacks**.

Workroom (US, costume shop): the space where the costumes are cut and constructed and fittings conducted.

Production Credits

Four productions have featured as case studies in this publication. They are listed below in alphabetical order.

Cinderella, adapted by Steve Marmion
Opened 25 November 2016
Oxford Playhouse, Oxford
Directed by Steve Marmion
Costumes designed by Amanda Hambleton
Costume supervision by Amanda Hambleton

The Deep Blue Sea, by Terence Rattigan
Opened 8 June 2016
The Lyttelton Theatre, National Theatre, South Bank, London
Directed by Carrie Cracknell
Set and costumes designed by Tom Scutt
Costume supervision by Lucy Martin

The Man of Mode, by Wycherley
Opened 12 May 2016
Meyrick Hall, Bournemouth
Directed by Luke Kergnahan
Set designed by Elle Pollock
Costumes designed by Emily Turner
Costume supervision by Maria Nicholson

The Women, by Clare Boothe Luce

Opened 23 October 2015

The Studio Theatre, Arts University Bournemouth

Directed by Gareth Corke

Set designed by Sam Edwards

Costume design by Rebecca Pride

Costume supervision by Milly Barter

Useful Addresses

The suppliers' list below preferences the United Kingdom, as this where I have experience. The suppliers from the United States have been principally sourced by scouring social media pages on the Internet and from speaking to a wonderful group of American professors who visited my institution in the summer of 2017 for a summer school under the tutelage of my colleagues Mandy Barrington and Wayne Martin. The United States is a very big place, and this list is intended to give an indication of suppliers that are rated as top-quality by costume professionals. The latest (and sadly, not that recent) publication detailing US suppliers is *The*

Useful Addresses 1 Fabric shops, Berwick Street, London

Photograph: Margaret Maguire.

New York Theatrical Sourcebook (2011–2012), produced by the Association of Theatrical Artists and Craftspeople, which includes resources for costume, wardrobe, prop rentals and fabrication, scenic arts and set construction, as well as general theatrical suppliers.

In the UK, suppliers are clustered in much smaller geographical areas, largely in London. I would advise costume supervisors to look closely at Facebook, pages including Costume Networking Group (which preferences the UK) and Costume People (which preferences the USA), and study the 'Recommendations' tabs on the left. These networks also offer direct and up-to-date recommendations to those who ask.

UNITED KINGDOM

FABRIC SUPPLIERS

A1 Fabrics

50/52 Goldhawk Road, Shepherd's Bush, London W12 8DH

020 8740 7349

Borovicks Fabrics Ltd

16 Berwick Street, London W1V 4HP

(fabrics, laces, trimmings)

www.borovickfabricsltd.co.uk

020 7437 2180/0520

Broadwick Silks

9–11 Broadwick Street, London W1F OBD

www.broadwicksilks.com

020 7734 3320

Classic Textiles

44 Goldhawk Road, Shepherd's Bush, London W12 8DH

www.classic-textiles.com

020 87433516

Cloth House

47 Berwick Street, London W1F 8SJ

www.clothhouse.com

020 7437 5155

Denholme Velvets Ltd

Halifax Road, Denholme, Bradford, West Yorkshire BD13 4EZ

www.denholme-velvets.co.uk

01274 832185

Derby House Fabrics

Greenside Lane, Bradford BD8 9TF

www.derbyhousefabrics.com

01274 360 550

Epra Fabrics Ltd

54 Brick Lane, London E1 6RH

(dress fabrics, velvets, linings)

www.eprafabrics.co.uk

020 7247 1248

Euro Japan Links Ltd

32 Nant Road, Childs Hill, London NW2 2AT

(sashiko fabrics, Japanese cottons, kimono pieces)

www.eurojapanlinks.com

020 8201 9324

Gallia Textiles

Stafford Industrial Estate, Hillman Close, Hornchurch RM11 2SJ

(duchesse satin, silks, brocades, nets, velvets)

www.galliatextiles.co.uk

01708 456 068

Graham Smith Fabrics Ltd

Bedes Close, James Street, Thornton, Bradfield, West Yorkshire BD13 3NR

(wool fabrics)

www.grahamsmithfabrics.com

01274 507022

Hainsworth & Sons Ltd (Wholesale)

Spring Valley Mills, Stanningley, Pudsey, West Yorkshire LS28 6DW

www.hainsworth.co.uk

0113 257 0391

Hansons Fabrics

Station Road, Sturminster Newton, Dorset DT10 1BD

www.hansonsfabrics.co.uk

01258 472698

Henry Bertrand

52 Holmes Road, London, NW5 3AB

(Chinese, Thai and Indian silks)

www.henrybertrand.co.uk

020 7424 7000

Joel & Son Fabrics

73–87 Church Street, London NW8 8EU

www.joelandsonfabrics.com

020 7724 6895

MacCulloch & Wallis

25–26 Poland Street, London W1F 8QN

(silk, bridal, tailoring, trimmings, millinery)

www.macculloch-wallis.co.uk

020 76290311

Mermaid Fabrics

364 Mare Street, Hackney, London E8 1HR

www.mermaidfabrics.co.uk

020 8985 3694

Whaleys (Bradford) Ltd

Harris Court, Great Horton, Bradford BD7 4EQ

(silk, cotton, linens, wools, canvas, calicos)

www.whaleys-bradford.ltd.uk

01274 576718

Wolfin Textiles Ltd

Unit 4, Phoenix Works, Cornwall Road, London HA5 4UH

(interlinings, calico, lawn, muslin etc.)

www.wolfintextiles.co.uk

020 8427 7429

DEPARTMENT STORE

Liberty

Regent Street, London W1B 5AH

(fabrics, buttons and trimmings)

www.libertylondon.com

020 7734 1234

SARI FABRIC SUPPLIERS

Aarti Sarees Ltd

22 South Road, Southall, Middlesex UB1 1RT

www.aartisaree.com

020 8571 4689

Bombay Stores

Bombay Buildings, Shearbridge Road, Bradford, West Yorkshire BD7 1NX

(the UK's largest Asian department store)

www.bombaystores.co.uk

01274 729993

DesiSaree

120a The Broadway, Southall, Middlesex UB1 1QF

www.desisarees.com

020 8843 1815

Punjab Textiles Ltd

3 Featherstone Road, Southall, Middlesex UB2 5AA

www.punjabtextileslondon.co.uk

020 8574 2059

WHOLESALE SILK SUPPLIERS

Bennett Silks

Crown Royal Park, Higher Hillgate, Stockport SK1 3HB

Email: info@bennett-silks.co.uk

www.bennett-silks.co.uk

0161 476 8600

James Hare Ltd

Monarch House, 7 Queen Street, Leeds LS1 2TW

(silks from Europe and the Far East)

www.james-hare.com

0113 2431 204

Pongees Ltd

Fountain House, 4 Chapel Place, Rivington Street, London EC2A 3DQ

Email: sales@pongees.co.uk

www.pongees.co.uk

020 7739 9130

LEATHER AND SUEDE

Alma Leather

Head Office: 12–14 Greatorex Street, London E1 5NF

Showroom: 8 Vigo Street, London W1S 3HJ

Email: sales@almahome.co.uk

www.alma1938.com

020 7377 0762

G.H. Leathers

Units D and E, Bury Close, Higham Ferrers, Northamptonshire NN10 8HQ

Email: sales@leathermerchants.com

www.leathermerchants.com

01933 311116

PLEATERS

F. Ciment (Pleating) Ltd

18a Station Close, Potters Bar, Hertfordshire EN6 1TL

Email: info@cimentpleating.co.uk

www.cimentpleating.co.uk

01707 661 311

RIBBONS AND TRIMMINGS (NOTIONS)

Barnett Lawson

16/17 Little Portland Street, London W1W 8NE

Email: info@bltrimmings.com

www.bltrimmings.com

0207 636 8591

Button Queen Ltd

76 Marylebone Lane, London W1U 2PR

(antique and modern buttons)

Email: information@thebuttonqueen.co.uk

www.thebuttonqueen.co.uk

020 7935 1505

Kleins

5 Noel Street, London W1F 8GD

www.kleins.co.uk

020 737 6162

MacCulloch & Wallis

25–26 Poland Street, London W1F 8QN

(trims, millinery supplies, ribbons, braids)

Samples and general enquiries, email: samples@macculloch.com

www.macculloch-wallis.co.uk

020 7629 0311

Ostrich Feather Manufacturing Co. Ltd

Foundry Road, Stamford, Lincolnshire PE9 2PP

(marabou yardage, ostrich trimming)

www.ostrichfeather.co.uk

01780 767895

Swarovski Optical

Unit 11, Perrywood Business Park, Honeycrock Lane, Salfords, Surrey RH1 5FJ

(rhinestone, pearlized and metallic-effect trimmings)

www.swarovski.com

01737 856812

BEADS

Beadworks

Covent Garden Bead Shop, 21a Tower Street, Covent Garden, London WC2H 9NS

www.beadworks.co.uk

020 7240 0931

Creative Beadcraft

1 Marshall Street, London W1F 9BA

www.creativebeadcraft.co.uk

020 7734 1982

HABERDASHERY

Devine & Co. Ltd

57a Brightwell Avenue, Westcliff on Sea, Essex SS0 9EB

(boning and corset laces)

Email: devinesupplies@aol.com

01702 352500 or 01702 613101

Vena Cava Design

PO Box 3597, Poole, Dorset BH14 9ZL

(corset components)

www.venacavadesign.co.uk

TAILORING SUPPLIES

Bernstein & Banleys Ltd

Unit 10, Britannia Business Park, Comet Way, Southend on Sea, Essex SS2 6GE

Email: shop@theliningcompany.co.uk

www.theliningcompany.co.uk

01702523315

REPLICA CLOTHING

Darcy Clothing

The Maltings, Castle Precints, Lewes, East Sussex BN7 1YT

(replica men's clothing, and some women's, 16th century–1950's)

Email: sales@darcyclothing.com

www.darcyclothing.com

01273 471586

House of Foxy

20th Century Clothiers Ltd,

1st Floor, Unit 4, Wellington Mills, Quebec Street, Elland, West Yorkshire HX5 9AS

www.thehouseoffoxy.com

01422 376461

THREADS

Madeira Threads (UK) Ltd

12 Hallikeld Close, Barker Business Park, Melmerby Ripon, North Yorkshire HG4 5GZ

(threads and fabric – mail order)

www.madeira.co.uk

01765 64170003

COSTUME SHOP EQUIPMENT

Morplan Ltd

56 Great Titchfield Street, London W1W 7DF

(pattern paper, plastic garment covers, coat hangers)

Email: web.support@morplan.com

www.morplan.com

020 7636 1887

CATERING UNIFORMS

Denny's

55a Dean Street, Soho, London W1D 6AG

or

62 Berners Street, London W1T 3NN

(chef and service clothing)

www.dennys.co.uk

020 7494 2745

Internet orders: 01372 377904

020 3815 2900

GLOVES

Dents

Warminster Business Park, Furnax Lane, Warminster, Wiltshire BA12 8PE

Email: sales@dents.co.uk

www.dents.co.uk

01985 212291

SHOES AND DANCEWEAR

Anello & Davide

15 St. Albans Grove, Kensington, London W8 5BP

(period shoes, bespoke)

www.handmadeshoes.co.uk

020 7938 2255

Dancia International

235 High Street, Crowthorne, Berkshire RG45 7AH

www.dancia.co.uk

01344 286884

Freeds

94 St. Martin's Lane, London WC2N 4AT

(dance/period shoes)

Email: shop@freed.co.uk

www.freedoflondon.com

020 7240 0432

Gandolfi

190 Mill Road, Wellingborough, Northants NN8 1PR

(dance shoes, tights, leotards)

info@gandolfi.co.uk

01933 224007

STOCKINGS – COTTON, WOOL AND SILK

Funn Hosiery Ltd

PO Box 102, Steyning, West Sussex BN44 3EB

(period replica tights and stockings)

www.FunnHosiery.co.uk

0870 8743866

WIGS

Derek Easton Wigs

1 Dorothy Avenue, Peacehaven, Essex BN10 8LP

Email: wigs@derekeastonwigs.co.uk

www.derekeastonwigs.co.uk

01273 588 262

Hairaisers

9–11 Sunbeam Road, Park Royal, London NW10 6JP

www.hairaisers.com

020 8965 2500

THEATRE MAKE-UP

Kryolan

22 Tavistock Street, Covent Garden, London WC2E 7PY

Email: info-uk@kryolan.com

www.kryolan.com

020 7240 3111

MAC Cosmetics

maccosmetics.co.uk

MILLINERY SUPPLIERS AND BLOCKS

Bates (Hatter)

73 Jermyn Street, London SW1Y 6NP

www.bates-hats.com

020 7734 4707

Boon & Lane Ltd

7–11 Taylor Street, Luton, Bedfordshire LU2 0EY

www.hatblockstore.co.uk

01582 723224

Herbert Johnson

7 Piccadilly Arcade, St. James, London SW1Y 6NH

(military hats and civilian headwear)

www.herbert-johnson.co.uk

020 7409 7277

Lock & Co. Hatters

6 St. James's Street, London SW1A 1EF

www.lockhatters.co.uk

020 7930 8874

DYES AND FABRIC PAINT AND CRAFT SUPPLIERS

Alec Tiranti

27 Warren Street, London W1T 5NB

(tools, materials and equipment for modelling/carving/sculpture)

www.tiranti.co.uk

020 7380 0808

Brodie and Middleton

30–31 Store Street, London WC1E 7QE

(paints, glues, brushes, leather sprays etc.)

Email: info@brodies.net

www.brodies.net

020 7836 7521

Colourcraft Ltd
(acrylic paints, marbling inks, gold and silver mix)
Email: enquiries@colourcraft-ltd.com
www.colourcraftltd.com
0114 242 1431

Daler Rowney Ltd
Peacock Lane, Bracknell, Berkshire RG12 8SS
(fine art and graphic materials)
www.daler-rowney.com
01344 4610000

Henkel Ltd
Wood Lane End, Hemel Hempstead, Hertfordshire HP2 4RQ
(Dylon fabric dyes and fabric paints)
www.dylon.co.uk
01442 278000

Matrix Composite Materials Company Ltd
2 Folly Lane, St. Philips, Bristol BS2 ORH
(liquid latex)
www.matrix-composites.co.uk
0117 9548040

Pentonville Rubber Products Ltd
104–106 Pentonville Road, London N1 9JB
(plastics and foam rubber)
www.pentonvillerubber.co.uk
020 7837 7553

Rainbow Silks
6 Wheelers Yard, High Street, Great Missenden, Buckinghamshire HP16 OAL
(silk painting and fabric decoration supplies and kits)
www.rainbowsilks.co.uk
01494 862111

COSTUME HIRE

Academy Costumes

50 Rushworth Street, London SE1 ORB

(main stock 1900's to 1980's)

Email: info@academycostumes.com

www.academycostumes.co.uk

020 7620 0771

Angels the Costumiers

1 Garrick Road, London NW9 6AA

(costume hire)

www.angels.uk.com

020 8202 2244

Fax: 020 8202 1820

Bristol Costume Services

Filwood House, Filwood Road, Bristol BS16 3RY

Email: bcsbristol@aol.com

www.bristolcostumeservices.com

0117 965 9555

Cosprop

469–475 Holloway Road, London N7 6LE

Email: enquiries@cosprop.com

www.cosprop.com

020 7561 7300

Fax: 020 7561 7310

Costume Hire Direct

Unit 2, New Buildings Farm, Winchester Road, Petersfield, Surrey GU32 3PB

www.costumehiredirect.co.uk

01730 239515

Flame Torbay Costume Hire

35 Market Street, Torquay, Devon TQ1 3AW

www.flametorbay.co.uk

01803 211930

History in the Making Ltd

4a Aysgarth Road, Waterlooville, Hampshire PO7 7UG

(historical reconstruction specialists)

Email: info@history-making.com

www.history-making.com

023 9225 3175

National Theatre Costume Hire

Brixton Road, London SW9 6DE

Email: costume_hire@nationaltheatre.org.uk

www.nationaltheatre.org.uk

020 7452 3970

Royal Exchange Manchester

Northern Quarter, 47–53 Swan Street, Manchester M4 5JY

Email: costume.hire@royalexchange.co.uk

www.royalexchange.co.uk/costumehire

0161 819 6660

RSC Costume Hire

The Other Place, Southern Lane, Stratford-upon-Avon, Warwickshire CV37 6BH

Email: costume.hire@rsg.org.uk

www.rsc.org.uk

01789 272444

ARMOUR

Bapty & Co. Ltd

Witley Gardens, Norwood Green, Middlesex UB2 4ES

(sword belts, holsters etc.)

www.bapty.co.uk

020 8574 7700

PROP COSTUME

Mahogany

28 High Street, Harlesden, London NW10 4LX

(carnival costumes)

Email: costumes@mahoganycarnival.com

www.mahoganycarnival.com

020 896 14446

Rainbow Productions

Unit 3, Greenlea Park, Prince George's Road, London SW19 2JD

(character costume specialists)

Email: info@rainbowproductions.co.uk

www.rainbowproductions.co.uk

020 8254 5300

HARNESSES AND FLY SPECIALISTS

Flying by Foy

Unit 4, Borehamwood Enterprise Centre, Theobald Street, Borehamwood, Hertfordshire WD6 4RQ

www.Flybyfoy.com/contact/

020 8236 0234

GUILDS, COUNCILS AND ASSOCIATIONS

Costume Society

150 Aldersgate Street, London EC1A 4AB

www.costumesociety.org.uk

Costume & Textile Study Centre

Shire Hall, Market Avenue, Norwich NR1 3JO

www.ctacostume.org.uk

01603 745766

Crafts Council

44a Pentonville Road, Islington, London N1 9BY

www.craftscouncil.org.uk

020 7806 2500

MUSEUMS AND RESEARCH

Fashion Research Centre

Fashion Museum, Assembly Rooms, Bennett Street, Bath BA1 2QH

Email: fashion_enquiries@bathnes.gov.uk

www.museumofcostume.co.uk

01225 477789

Imperial War Museum

Lambeth Road, London SE1 6HZ

www.iwm.org.uk

020 7416 5000

National Theatre Archive

The Cut, Lambeth, London SE1 8LL

or

Brixton Road, London SW9 6DE

www.nationaltheatre.org.uk

020 7452 3135

Victoria and Albert Museum

Cromwell Road, London SW7 2RL

www.vam.ac.uk

020 3666 2043

UNITED STATES

FABRIC SUPPLIERS

Blue Moon Fabrics

305 E. 9th Street, #110-112, Los Angeles CA 90015

www.bluemoonfabrics.com

Fabrics and Fabrics

270 West 38th Street, Floor 3, New York NY 10018

www.fabrics-fabrics.com

1-212-391-7777

Fishman's Fabrics

1101 South Desplaines Street, Chicago IL 60607

www.fishmansfabrics.com

1-312-922-7250

Ginny's Fine Fabrics

211 South Broadway, Rochester MN 55904

www.ginnysfinefabrics.com

1-507-285-9134

Jo-Ann Stores

LLC, 5555 Darrow Road, Hudson OH 44236

(fabric stores throughout the USA and online)

www.joann.com/stores

1-888-739-4120

Metro Textiles Corp.

265 West 37th Street, Room 908, New York NY 10018

www.metrotextile.blogspot.co.uk

1-212-209-0004

Michael Levine Inc.

920 Maple Avenue, Los Angeles CA 90015

www.LowPriceFabric.com

1-213-622-6259

Mood Designer Fabrics

225 West 37th Street, 3rd Floor, New York NY 10018

1-212-730-5003

or

1726 West Pico Blvd, Los Angeles CA 90015
www.moodfabrics.com
1-323-653-6663

Rosen & Chadick Fabrics
108 West 39th Street, Floor 13, New York NY 10018
www.rosenandchadickfabrics.com
1-212-869-0142

Shannon Fabrics
3131 South Alameda Street, Los Angeles CA 90058
www.shannonfabrics.com
1-323-234-5252

SR Harris Fabric Outlet
8865 Zealand Avenue North, Brookyn Park MN 55445
or
3715 West Highway 13, Burnsville MN 55337
www.srharrisfabric.com
1-763-424-3500

Textile Discount Outlet
2121 West 21st Street, Chicago IL 60608
www.textilediscountoutlet.com
1-773-847-0572

LEATHER AND SUEDE

Leather Impact
525 7th Avenue, Floor 10, Suite 1012, New York NY 10018
www.leatherimpact.com
1-212-302-2332

WIGS

Wigboys

1390 North McDowell Boulevard, Suite G-210, Petaluma CA 94954

www.wigboys.com

1-707-763-1978

MAKE-UP SUPPLIERS

Ben Nye Co. Inc.

3655 Lenawee Avenue, Los Angeles CA 90016

www.bennye.com

1-310-839-1984

Kryolan

132 9th Street, San Francisco CA 94103-2603

www.kryolan.com

1-800 579-6526

REPLICA CLOTHING

Fall Creek Suttlery

PO Box 92 Whitestown IA 46075

(American Civil War clothing, Victorian clothing and accessories)

www.fcsutler.com

1-765-482-1861

Period Corsets

10002 Aurora Avenue N#36, Seattle WA 98133

(source for period corsets, petticoats 1560–1912)

www.periodcorsets.com

1-206-264-0997

Townsends

PO Box 415, 133 North 1st Street, Pierceton IN 46562

(reproduction clothing and accessories 1750–1840)

www.townsends.us

1-800-338-1665

HABERDASHERY

Corset Making Supplies.com

Delicious, LLC, 212 East Girard Avenue, Philadelphia PA 19125

www.corsetmaking.com

1-215-413-8259

Farthingales

3306 Pico Boulevard, Santa Monica CA 90405

www.farthingalesla.com

1-310-392-1787

Richard the Thread

1960 South La Cienega Boulevard, Los Angeles CA 90034

www.richardthethread.com

1-310-837-4997

COSTUME HIRE

TDF Costume Collection

3412 Level, Suite 1, 36th Street, Astoria NY 11106

(collection of 80,000 costumes from Broadway shows for rent)

www.tdf.org

1-212-989-5855

Western Costume Co.

11041 Vanowen Street, North Hollywood, Los Angeles CA 91605

www.westerncostume.com

1-816-760-0900

SHOES AND DANCEWEAR

Capezio

Head Office: 1 Campus Road, Totowa NJ 07512

(dancewear, tights and shoes)

www.capezio.com

1-973-595-9000

Chacott

20 East 20th Street, New York NY 10003

(dance/period shoes)

www.freedusa.com

1-212-432-4416

HARNESSES AND FLY SPECIALISTS

Flying by Foy

3275 East Patrick Lane, Las Vegas NV 89120

www.flybyfoy.com/contact/

1-702-454-3500

GUILDS, COUNCILS AND ASSOCIATIONS

Association of Theatrical Artists and Craftspeople

48 Fairway Street, Bloomfield NJ 07003

www.atacbiz.com and Facebook

1-212-563-5830

Costume Society of America

PO Box 852, Columbus GA 31902-0852

www.costumesocietyamerica.com

1-706-615-2851

United States Institute for Theatre Technology

315 South Crouse Avenue, Suite 200, Syracuse NY 13210

(the trade association for the theatre and live entertainment production communities)

www.usitt.org

1-800-938-7488

MUSEUMS AND RESEARCH

Fashion Institute of Technology

227 West 27th Street, New York NY 10001

www.fitnyc.edu/museum

1-212-217-4558

Metropolitan Museum of Art

1000 5th Avenue, New York NY 10028

www.metmuseum.org

1-212-535-7710

EUROPE

FABRIC SUPPLIERS

Fucotex Fabrics and Lace

Fucotex, Burgfriedenstrasse 23, 86316 Friedberg, Germany

www.fucotex.de/en.html

0821 263800

COSTUME HIRE

Atelier de la Colombe

32 rue faubourg de Pierre, 67000 Strasbourg, France

03 88 22 17 81

Sommier et Fils

3 pass Brady, 75010 Paris, France

www.Sommier.com

01 42 08 27 01

Tirelli Costumi

Via Pompeo Magno, 11/b, 00192 Roma, Italy

(costume atelier and hire house for theatre and film)

www.tirellicostumi.com

06 321 1201

Bibliography

Association of Theatrical Artists and Craftspeople. *The New York Theatrical Sourcebook.* Louisville, KY: Broadway Press, 2011–2012.

Barrington, M. *Stays and Corsets: Historical Patterns Translated for the Modern Body*. New York: Focal Press, 2015.

Brennan, C. 'Are women getting any closer to equality in theatre?', *The Guardian*, 6 March 2012. Available at: https://www.theguardian.com/stage/theatreblog/2012/mar/06/women-equality-theatre (accessed 16 March 2018).

Clancy, D. *Designing Costume for Stage and Screen*. London: Batsford, 2014.

Clapp, S. 'The Deep Blue Sea review – an explosive revival', *The Guardian*, 12 June 2016.

Coffey-Webb, L. *Managing Costume Collections*. Lubbock, TX: Texas Tech University Press, 2016.

Holmes, S. *National Theatre Costume*. London: National Theatre Publications, 2014.

Holt, M. *A Phaidon Theatre Manual: Costume and Make-up*. New York: Phaidon, 1988.

Howard, P. *What is Scenography?* 2nd ed., New York: Routledge, 2009.

Ingham, R. *From Page to Stage*. Portsmouth, NH: Heinemann 1998.

Ingham, R., and Covey, L. *The Costumer's Handbook.* Englewood Cliffs, NJ: Prentice Hall, 1980.

Ingham, R., and Covey, L. *The Costume Designer's Handbook*. Portsmouth, NH: Heinemann, 1992.

Ingham, R., and Covey, L. *The Costume Technician's Handbook*. Portsmouth, NH: Heinemann, 1992.

Jackson, S. *Costumes for the Stage*. London: A&C Black, 2001.

Kincman, L. *The Stage Manager's Toolkit*. New York: Focal Press, 2013.

Kucharski, J. *Tyranny of Style*. Available at: http://tyrannyofstyle.com/about (accessed 16 March 2018).

La Motte, R. *Costume Design 101: The Art and Business of Costume Design for Film and Television*. Studio City, CA: Michael Wiese, 2001.

Malloy, K.E. *The Art of Theatrical Design*. New York: Focal Press, 2015.

McKeown, L. *Do Lead – Share Your Vision. Inspire Others. Achieve the Impossible*. London: The Do Book Company, 2014.

McMills, A.E. *The Assistant Lighting Designer's Toolkit*. New York: Focal Press, 2014.

Nandoolman Landis, D. *Costume Design*. Waltham, MA: Focal Press, 2012.

Pavelka, M. *So You Want to Be a Theatre Designer?* London: Nick Hern Books, 2015.

Perry, P. (Ed.). *The Vogue Sewing Book of Fitting, Adjustments, and Alterations*. New York: Butterick Fashion Marketing, 1972.

Shoben, M.M. and Ward, J.P. *Pattern Cutting and Making Up: The Professional Approach*. Oxford: Heinemann Professional Publishing, 1987.

Smith, A. *The Sewing Book*. London: Dorling Kindersley, 2013.

Tempest, F. *The Feminization of the Costume Department in the British Film and Television Industry*. Bournemouth: Arts University Bournemouth, 2011.

West, N., McClean, V., and Stender, M. (Eds). *Costume Symposium 2006*. Bournemouth: The Arts Institute, 2006.

Author Biography

Rebecca Pride graduated with her first degree in Drama and Theatre Studies from Royal Holloway College, London University. She followed this with postgraduate study as a theatre designer at the Slade School of Fine Art, graduating in 1988. Rebecca spent 15 years working as a designer in the professional theatre, working on over 100 projects, some as diverse as *The Bacchae of Euripides*, Joe Orton's *What the Butler Saw*, and *Three Steps to Heaven*, a musical rendition of the Buddy Holly story. Rebecca was also fortunate enough to work in a variety of different performance spaces, from the tiny Gate Theatre in Notting Hill to the grandeur of the main proscenium arch space at Theatr Clwyd in North Wales. After 20 years in the theatre industry, Rebecca joined the Arts University Bournemouth in 2005, becoming Course Leader and Senior Lecturer for the BA (Hons) Costume and Performance Design course in 2009.

Rebecca believes passionately in an experiential method of teaching. As a result, she has developed a curriculum within the course that allows students to take part in a wide variety of 'live projects' with external theatre and film companies and other complementary courses at the Arts University. The course is unique in the UK for delivering teaching in four distinct areas of practice that can lead to 'named awards' in Scenography, Costume Design for Screen, Costume Supervision and Costume Interpretation. Although Rebecca has worked largely as a designer throughout her career, costume supervision has always been a strong interest and focus for her, and formally describing the process of supervising in the classroom, as well as in written form in this book, has been a fascinating exercise.

Her recent work as a film producer includes *Wimbledon 1936–1937*, *Storytelling from an Original Point of View*, *These Days*, *Reverie*, *La Passarella* and *Past, Presently*. Theatre Design includes productions of *The Women* by Clare Boothe Luce, *The Threepenny Opera* by Brecht, *La Ronde* by Schnitzler, Abi Morgan's *Tender* and Andrew Louden's *Mary Barton*.

Her exhibition curation credits include *A Stitch in Line*, *West Side 360°* and *Drawing Theatre: Pamela Howard*. Rebecca edited and designed a highly acclaimed publication to accompany the latter exhibition, also entitled *Drawing Theatre: Pamela Howard* (a Text+Work publication).

In recognition of the quality of work the staff and students have achieved in recent years, Rebecca's course was presented with the prestigious Queen's Anniversary Prize for Higher and Further Education (The Twelfth Round 2016–2018) for excellence in Costume Design – a bi-annual award that is the personal gift of Her Majesty Queen Elizabeth.

Index

M

N

O

P

U

V

W

Y